MISTRUST

HAU
BOOKS

www.haubooks.com

THE MALINOWSKI MONOGRAPHS

In tribute to the foundational, yet productively contentious, nature of the ethnographic imagination in anthropology, this series honors the creator of the term "ethnographic theory" himself. Monographs included in this series represent unique contributions to anthropology and showcase groundbreaking work that contributes to the emergence of new ethnographically-inspired theories or challenge the way the "ethnographic" is conceived today.

MISTRUST
AN ETHNOGRAPHIC THEORY

Matthew Carey

Hau Books
Chicago

© 2017 Hau Books and Matthew Carey

Cover, ink wash painting by BadaShanren (Zhu Da)

Cover and layout design: Sheehan Moore

Typesetting: Prepress Plus (www.prepressplus.in)

ISBN: 978-0-9973675-2-2
LCCN: 2017934092

Hau Books
Chicago Distribution Center
11030 S. Langley
Chicago, IL 60628
www.haubooks.com

Hau Books is marketed and distributed by The University of Chicago Press.
www.press.uchicago.edu

Printed in the United States of America on acid-free paper.

ꡕ ⵙ ꡀꡪꡖ, ꡑ ꡈꡪⵙꡋ. ⵙꡓꡥ ꡙ ꡀꡖⵙ

"For Si Lahsen, the slipperiest of fishes. Friend and teacher."

Table of contents

Acknowledgments   xi
Note on transliteration   xiii

Introduction: The apotheosis of trust   1

CHAPTER I
Lying and obfuscation: The uncertain ground of speech   15

CHAPTER 2
Trust or tolerance? On the treachery of friends   39

CHAPTER 3
The triumph of contingency: Anarchism as Realpolitik   63

CHAPTER 4
Conspiracy, witchcraft and theft: Manifestations of the
mistrusting imagination   85

Conclusion   107

References   111
Index   125

Acknowledgments

This text, like all ethnography (but more so), is an exercise in betrayal of the people who inspired it: my friends and acquaintances in the Moroccan High Atlas. I trust they will forgive me in time. Particular gratitude and apologies are owed Si Lahsen, Sabira, Si Bou Jmā' and Si Morad, in conversation with whom I developed most of the ideas of mistrust presented here. Without them, nothing.

Professional thanks are due to Olivier Allard, Vera Skvirskaja, Susan Whyte, Luc Boltanski, Arnaud Esquerre, Inger Sjørslev, and Andrew Carey, who all read all or part of the text, as well as to the two anonymous reviewers, who greatly strengthened my argument, and to my editor, Giovanni da Col. Vera and Olivier must be thanked again: she for providing much of the online Ukrainian ethnography that features in chapter 4, and he for his part in developing some of the ideas concerning trust and mistrust that feature in the introduction (Rachel Renault also deserves thanks on this score). Much of the gestational work behind this thematic orientation had previously been accomplished while I was a visiting scholar in Paris in 2012–13. My stay was funded by the Collège de France and facilitated by Philippe Descola—to them and to the rest of my colleagues, I am grateful.

Finally, I would like to thank Charlotte Rosenmejer, whose redoubtable efficiency meant I had the time and mental space to write this book.

It goes without saying that where I err, the fault is mine: I should have checked; and where the argument is flawed, the fault is also mine: I should have thought a little harder.

Note on transliteration

All transliterations from the Russian or Arabic are standard. There is no one standardized system for transliterating Tashelhiyt into Latin script. As this is not a linguistically-minded publication, I have opted to make it as readable as possible for a non-specialist by following the more familiar Arabic transcription system. The following sounds have no standard English equivalent:

gh—a voiced ulular fricative, like a rolled French r
kh—a voiceless ulular fricative, like the ch in 'loch'
q—a deep glottal stop
r—a Spanish rolled r
'—a voiced epiglottal, like retching

Other conventions include:
ay—a diphthong, as in 'eye'
i—a long vowel, as in 'sheep'
j—a soft French j

All proper nouns and common nouns are spelled without diacritics.

Without the general trust that people have in each other, society itself would disintegrate
Georg Simmel

If you once forfeit the confidence of your fellow citizens, you can never regain their respect and esteem
Abraham Lincoln

Trust is the glue of life. It's the most essential ingredient in effective commu-nication. It's the foundational principle that holds all relationships
Stephen. R. Covey (management guru)

Trust is what makes contracts, plans and everyday transactions possible; it facilitates the democratic process… It is essential for our lives. It is trust, more than money, that makes the world go round
Joseph Stiglitz (economist)

You must trust and believe in people, or life becomes impossible
Anton Chekhov

Whatever matters to human beings, trust is the atmosphere in which it thrives
Sissela Bok (philosopher)

If you cannot trust yourself, you cannot even trust your mistrust of yourself—so that without this underlying trust in the whole system of nature you are simply paralyzed
Alan. W. Watts (Californian philosopher-guru)

Trusting ought to be a human right
Jacques Attali (French politician)

When you learn to trust in trust, then you become confident
Jean-Claude van Damme (actor)

Introduction
The apotheosis of trust

There is perhaps no concept that so federates the disparate caucuses of modernity as trust. From the broad plains of popular psychology to the narrow marches of academia, from the semantic metastasis of management-speak to the quiet, curatorial passion of established religion, trust is everywhere. And everywhere it is lauded as both necessary and good. Necessary, in that trust is, simply put, a precondition for virtually all aspects of collective human existence. So each of the human and social sciences separately insists that their very object of study depends on the presence of trust. For sociologists like Simmel, trust is the glue of society: we could not live alongside others without the minimal trust that allows us periodically to turn our backs to them. For economists, trust is the foundation upon which almost all economic transactions are built; for political scientists, it is the cornerstone of legitimacy and the *fons et origo* of government. And, in the wake of Grice's pragmatic philosophy, trust is even frequently described as a condition of speech and communication.

This fairly incontrovertible claim of necessity is customarily seconded by a moral claim of virtue. As the Swedish-American philosopher Sissela Bok (1978) puts it, whatever it is we value, trust enables it to flourish. Trust, particularly extensive social trust, is variously depicted as enhancing the social fabric, lowering crime rates, increasing happiness, promoting development, generating prosperity, improving one's sex life, and fostering mutually beneficial relationships. Beginning with Weber's foundational work on the legal structures, social forms, and cultural configurations that progressively allow for the extension of credit beyond the immediate family circle and so give rise to modernity, vast scholarly resources have thus been deployed to identify the processes and institutions that enable trust. Underpinning much of this literature is the assumption that trust is, broadly speaking, a good thing for both the individual and the community that enjoy it, be they paupers, peasants, princes, or thieves. And the more we have of it, the better. Of course, this correlation is not infinitely extensible: everybody recognizes that at some point trust tips over into credulity and this can have unfortunate consequences, but the general rule holds. Trust must be maximized.

There is, unsurprisingly, little room within this absolutist framework for a nuanced discussion of mistrust. With few exceptions (e.g. Rosanvallon 2006), it is treated as little more than an absence of trust—just as in classical Augustinian theodicy, evil does not have an identity in its own right but is a mere privation of goodness. As such, mistrust is frequently not seen as doing anything but *undo* the positive work of trust. Where trust builds relationships, mistrust sunders them; where trust breeds wealth, mistrust generates poverty; where trust gives rise to effective communication and extensive social ties, mistrust is the mother of confusion and isolation. Mistrust is, in short, uniquely corrosive of human bonds—it is social acid. It is precisely this idea that was developed in the literature on "lower-trust" societies that briefly blossomed in the heyday of peasant studies, from the 1950s to the 1970s. The classic work is Banfield's *The moral basis of a backwards society* (1958), in which the inhabitants of the pseudonymous village of Montegrano, in the Italian *Mezzogiorno*, are depicted as chronically and cripplingly suspicious of everybody outside their immediate nuclear family.[1] They lie, gossip, backstab, and betray without compunction, because they have no ethical ties beyond those of kinship. This is the dog-eat-dog world of so-called amoral familism, in which mistrust locks people and societies into a vicious cycle of backwardness and underdevelopment as squalid and unrelenting as a world without sunlight.

I have spent several years living in and then visiting a peasant society in the Moroccan High Atlas, which shares many of the key characteristics identified

---

1.   Recognizably related lines of thought are developed by George Foster, who argued that peasant societies typically share a cognitive orientation towards an Image of Limited Good and the idea that success can only come at the expense of others, thus leading to mistrust (1965: 297), and Aguilar, who looks at how Mexican peasants seek to overcome an "ingrained disposition" toward mistrust (1984: 3). See Govier (1997) for an overview.

by Banfield: chronic and very vocal mistrust; communicative strategies based on obfuscation and dissembling; relentless gossiping; and frequent accusations of deceit and betrayal. My friends and interlocutors were adamant that "there is no trust" (*ur tilli tiqqa*); the minimal trust previously identified as necessary for human society was of course present, but it did not have the same social, discursive, or ideological extension as we might find in, say, Denmark, where I now live, or rural 1950s Utah, which Banfield uses as the foil for his analysis of Montegrano. And yet, despite these similarities, I cannot recognize Banfield's description of a chaotic Hobbesian world of solitude, anomie, and pitiless mutual predation. Certainly, the High Atlas lacks the structures of communication, practices of friendship, and political and economic institutions found in so-called high-trust societies. But it is not that there are simply *less* of these things; it is rather that those they have are different. This, I suspect, may be equally true of other societies characterized by widespread mistrust, such as the contemporary Ukraine, where I have since spent some time.[2]

Simmel describes trust as "a hypothesis regarding future behavior, a hypothesis certain enough to serve as a basis for practical conduct" and suggests that people, eras, and societies differ by the particular admixture of knowledge and ignorance that suffices to generate trust (1950: 318–19). In other words, the morphology of the trust hypothesis shapes and produces particular social forms. I argue that just the same is true of mistrust. It is an alternative hypothesis and one that gives rise to social forms of its own. These are not merely the photographic negative of those produced by trust, but interesting and occasionally admirable constructs in their own right. This book thus examines the impact of mistrust-qua-hypothesis on practices of conversation and communication, friendship and society, as well as politics and cooperation. To explore the nature of this hypothesis, we need to take a brief dip into the trust literature.

TRUST AS ATTITUDE, FAMILIARITY, AND CONTROL

The vast and near perfect concert of voices singing the praises of trust should not be mistaken for any unity of content. Trust may be necessary and it may be good, but it is far from clear precisely what it is. Indeed, for a long time it went

---

2.   I was in Odessa for three months in 2007, and returned to the Ukraine for follow-up visits in 2012 and 2013.

largely without saying. Though trust occupied a central position in the classical sociology of Max Weber, Talcott Parsons, Gabriel Tarde, and to a lesser extent Émile Durkheim,[3] it was rarely interrogated directly, functioning instead as a sort of black box at the heart of social theory. It is only in the work of Simmel that trust is tackled head on, but though his writings on the topic demonstrate his invariable ability to identify the crux of an issue, they run to fewer than ten pages in total[4] and failed to produce any significant intellectual progeny, at least in the short term. We have to wait until the 1960s and 1970s for the arrival of a wave of thinkers who transform trust into a central object of sociological reflection.

When they did so, they approached the topic from a wide variety of angles. One example is Garfinkel's notorious "breaching experiments" (1963), in which he encouraged his students to expose the unspoken expectations of social interactions by acting as if they were a lodger when visiting their parental home or behaving as if they assumed their interlocutor had hidden motives. These experiments addressed the implicit forms of trust that structure everyday interaction. Game theory, meanwhile, which explores decision-making in highly artificial environments, examines trust as a possible strategy in cooperation games like the (iterated) prisoner's dilemma (e.g. Axelrod 1984; Poundstone 1992).[5] In so doing, it is one of the rare fields to treat mistrust as anything other than a malediction;[6] in game theory, it can also be a rational strategy in just the same way as trust. Finally, Niklas Luhmann's highly influential *Trust and power*

---

3. The relevant texts are *The theory of social and economic organisation* (Weber 1947), *Action theory and the human condition* (Parsons 1978), *Psychologie économique* (Tarde 1902), and *La division du travail social* (Durkheim 1893).

4. I am indebted to Guido Möllering (2002) for counting them and also for providing a concise and thorough examination of Simmel's position.

5. For those unfamiliar with the prisoner's dilemma, it involves two criminal accomplices arrested by the police and placed in solitary confinement. The police lack evidence for the principal charge, but can convict on a lesser one; they separately offer the prisoners a choice: they can betray their partner or keep shtum. If they both hold their tongue, then they both serve one year; if they both betray the other, they both serve two years; and if one betrays the other and the other stays silent, then the traitor walks free whilst his unfortunate accomplice serves three years. The idea is to explore the different possible strategies to adopt in such a situation and people's reasons for doing so.

6. The other great exception is certain branches of political theory, which argue that democracy is predicated on a healthy mistrust of one's leaders (see chapter 3).

(1979), which builds on the foundational writings of Simmel, focuses on the functional aspects of trust as a means of simplifying the dizzying complexity of reality and thus opening up the possibility of further-reaching forms of action. Each of these approaches has given rise to huge and highly diverse bodies of literature that are largely immune to summary, although there has been no shortage of attempts to do so.[7] My purpose here is not to swell their ranks, but simply to develop a few points that are critical for understanding the approach to mistrust developed in this book.

First, is the opposition between trust as strategy and trust as a psychological state or attitude. Strategic approaches predominate in mainstream economics, where rational actors are the lynchpins of social analysis, as well as in the voluminous self-help and management literature, which broadly shares this vision of the human subject. In both cases, the decision to place one's trust in another is seen as a deliberate and conscious strategy that can be used to maximize success, however defined. The sociological and psychological literature, in contrast, tends to stress the attitudinal quality of trust. This takes a variety of forms: in psychology there is a clear contrast between dispositional approaches, which focus on people's general assumptions about the trustworthiness of others and interpersonal approaches, where trust is a function of a particular relationship (cf. Simpson 2007); in sociology, the situation is more complex, but in simple terms, one can identify a spectrum of foci ranging from personal trust to extensive social trust in unknown others (e.g., Putnam et al. 1993) or trust in the system (Seligman 1997), for instance the legal system.[8] These distinctions are hard fought, but what matters for our purposes here is that all of these different psychological and sociological perspectives stress that trust is not merely a matter of choice.[9] It is also a way of viewing the world.

---

7. Among the most straightforwardly and ambitiously titled are: Gambetta's pioneering edited volume, *Trust: Making and breaking cooperative relations* (1988); Fukuyama's *Trust: The social virtues and the creation of prosperity* (1995); Misztal's *Trust in modern societies* (1996); Seligman's *The problem of trust* (1997); Sztompka's *Trust: A sociological theory* (1999); Cook's edited volume, *Trust in society* (2001); Hardin's multiple contributions, including *Trust and trustworthiness* (2004) and *Trust* (2006); and Cofta's *Trust, complexity and control* (2007).

8. The original opposition elaborated by Luhmann is between personal trust and "system trust" or "system confidence" (*Systemvertrauen*), where the latter encompasses both faith in the system and in unknown others qua "personal systems" (1979: 22).

9. Indeed, Hardin (2001: 11) goes so far as to suggest that it is not about choice at all. The choice lies in the decision of whether or not to act on trust.

Second, this way of viewing the world is one that relies on familiarity as a basis for simplification. Luhmann points out that trust involves a telescoping of present and future. At any given moment, the social actor is necessarily confronted with infinitely ramifying possible futures. This vertiginous perspective is basically unmanageable for a human mind. Trust simplifies it, by functionally limiting these possible futures—"to show trust is to anticipate the future. It is to behave as though the future were certain" (1979: 10). For instance, if I can trust my business partner to deliver a shipment of goods for a particular date, then I can rent storage space, arrange meetings with potential buyers, and so forth. In other words, trust generates a temporal collapse, bringing the future into the present and vice versa. Simply put, trust amounts to confidence in one's expectations, and such expectations cannot emerge *ab nihilo*, but must depend on a certain degree of familiarity with either people, the world, or systemic representations of the real. At an interpersonal level, this simplification through familiarity expresses itself in the attribution of personalities to people (1979: 41); we interpret the behavior of others as motivated and synthesize these motivations into a character, which allows us to predict their behavior. Similar processes can be seen to be at work in socially extensive or system trust, which rely on simplifying models and a goodly degree of apophenia—the human tendency to see system, pattern, and intentions where there is only "noise." All these forms of trust also depend on the fundamental hypothesis identified by Simmel: "that there exists between our idea of a being and the being itself a definite connection and unity" (1990: 179). In other words, we must believe that other people or entities have durable personalities or characters, that we can understand them, and finally that we can faithfully represent them to ourselves.

Third, trust is, in the words of Dunn, "a policy for handling the freedom of other human agents or agencies" (1988: 75). We cannot have trust in entirely natural entities or systems because they have no agency: we do not, for example, trust the sun to rise or a tree to grow (cf. Sztompka 1999: 20).[10] Nor can we use the word trust to describe situations of complete predictability. There always has to be an element of risk. This umbilical relationship between trust and risk partly explains the current vitality of the trust literature. Trust, for a variety of mutually contradictory reasons, is frequently identified as a specifically modern concern. So on the one hand, in some of the more synthetic sociological literature, complex modern societies, where people freely choose with whom to

---

10. Though we may trust in God (an agent) to cause them to rise and grow respectively.

associate, are sharply contrasted with small-scale "traditional" societies, where kinship dominates; and both kinship and tradition are portrayed as a matter not of choice, but of duty or obligation (cf. Seligman 1997: 36; Sztompka 1999: 45). In such contexts, where behavior is not chosen, but determined by one's social role, there is supposedly little place or need for trust. Elsewhere, however, these same traditional networks of kinship and community are seen as the very basis for interpersonal trust (e.g. Putnam 2000; Algan et al. 2012), which modern society is progressively losing. In short, we are living in times where there is less and less trust, or perhaps more and more of it, but either way, everyone agrees that there is more need for it than ever (Giddens 1990).

In an increasingly disembodied and dislocated world, in which traditional forms of social control no longer apply and risk is the order of the day (Beck 1992), trust becomes *the* central social technology. If my local ironmonger sells me a dodgy trowel, I can simply take it back; but if I buy a dodgy Chinese trowel on an online auction site from a middleman in Surinam, then trust is all I have: trust in the Chinese factory, in the Surinamese middleman, in the site administrators, in the online payment system, in the postal service, and in the overarching legal framework. The relationship between trust and risk also high-lights the fact that trusting somebody always implies a degree of dependency (Marzano 2010) and, I would add, a *redistribution of control*. In trusting, we both relinquish control over our environment and attempt to extend control over others. If I trust my daughter to play in the yard and not stray into the street, I both abandon direct control over the situation and simultaneously try to assert control over her. Because if she does stray, then my trust will be withdrawn and she will no longer be allowed out on her own. Trust, in other words, is a rather absolute and unforgiving social technology: it requires compliance from those we trust, lest it be lost, perhaps forever. So much for trust. What of its shadow?

THE HYPOTHESIS OF MISTRUST

For the purposes of this book, we can think of mistrust as the countervailing hypothesis to that outlined above. It, too, is not simply a strategy or a matter of choice, but also a disposition and it is this aspect of the phenomenon that principally concerns me. People's grounds for deciding particular others are un-trustworthy have already been thoroughly explored in strategic analyses of trust; here the emphasis is on their reasons for assuming a *general attitude* of mistrust and the social implications of such an attitude. This also explains my choice of the term "mistrust" over "distrust": whilst the two are very close in meaning, distrust is more likely to be based on a specific past experience, whereas mistrust describes a general sense of the unreliability of a person or thing.

This general attitude of mistrust can, I suggest, be seen as rooted in the idea that familiarity is insufficient ground for trust.[11] Proximity and familiarity do not necessarily equate to knowability or certainty and cannot be used as a basis for generating expectations and predicting future behavior. This point is critical, for it directly challenges the very widespread notion that there is an umbilical relationship between the holy trinity of proximity, familiarity, and trust—a notion that reaches far beyond the literature specifically dedicated to the question. It is, as we have seen, the key contention of Banfield's work on the social implications of mistrust in Mediterranean societies, and it is also implicit in another disciplinary avenue of enquiry that sinks its roots into Mediterranean and Middle Eastern ethnography: the anthropology of hospitality. As Candea and da Col baldly state in their recent discussion of the question, "For Pitt-Rivers (1968: 20), as for Derrida, the stranger is the absolute unknown, whose radical alterity echoes the numinous presence of the divine itself. Hospitality emerges as a mechanism for holding this dangerous being in abeyance" (2012: 6). In other words, hospitality serves to neutralize the radical otherness of the stranger/guest and thus helps manage what Herzfeld, writing in a Cretan context, calls the "conventional distrust of *kseni* (outsiders)" (1987: 76). What is true of Crete is also true, to an extent, of much of the wider Mediterranean area,[12] of which the Moroccan High Atlas is in this respect a peripheral, but nonetheless vital, appendage. The category of strangers or outsiders (*ayt birra*) is one that can, depending on context, be effortlessly extended to describe everybody from residents of a nearby village, to foreigners proper. And all of these types of stranger are figures that may arouse suspicion and that represent, in any case, a potential threat: they are potentially untrustworthy.

---

11. There is, in fact, an alternative possible foundation for an absence of trust—viz. the assumption that the other is potentially knowable, but his intentions are malign (cf. Allard et al. 2016). This, however, can only, I suspect, really function as a basis for distrust of specific individuals; it is hard to see how it could be extended to a generalized attitude of mistrust without causing irreparable psychological harm. It is not, in any case, the object of this book.

12. As, indeed, in segmentary systems more generally.

The crucial point, however, is that they are not, at least in my experience, primarily untrustworthy *by virtue* of being strangers. If familiarity is, as I have suggested, insufficient grounds for trust, then it stands to reason that the straightforward unfamiliarity of strangers is not, in itself, a reason for mistrusting the other. Indeed, while most people in the High Atlas very vocally insist that they prefer the company of intimates (kinsmen, fellow villagers, or fellow tribesmen—i.e. people who are not "outsiders," *ayt birra*), and this preference is reflected in their behavior, nobody ever suggested to me that this was because strangers were less trustworthy. Indeed, unlike in Banfield's Montegrano, expressions of mistrust were just as commonly directed at close friends and family.[13] If people preferred to be among intimates, it was because one can only truly be at ease with one's own. So, if simple alterity is not the basis for this ideology of mistrust, on what foundation does it rest? Here it is perhaps instructive to turn once more to Simmel. In his classic piece on the topic, Simmel suggests that whilst the stranger is principally defined by the fact that he is a "potential wanderer" whose social position is a function of the fact that he came from the outside (1950: 402), he is also a stranger insofar as "one has only certain more general qualities in common [with him]" (1950: 405). And, he continues, "a trace of strangeness in this sense easily enters into even the most intimate relationships" (1950: 406), as no human bond can be pure specificity, devoid of more general, abstract qualities. Thus, strangeness transcends the stranger and seeps into all elements of social life.

Now, Simmel's definition of strangeness as wandering and generalizability makes little sense in an Atlassian context, but his dual understanding of the concept is worth retaining. For the people I worked with, outsiders (*ayt birra*) were primarily defined not by the fact of their external origin,[14] but by the fact that they were *socially* unknown. There was also, however, a second form of strangeness or

---

13. This is not to suggest that the people I lived and worked with simply failed to distinguish between intimates and strangers when it came to trusting them. Close social relations with kith and kin do of course require a greater degree of trust than that typically accorded unknown outsiders: one sleeps alongside them, entrusts property to them, etc. But crucially, people also made it clear that friends and family were also in some ways radically untrustworthy as well.

14. Indeed, some anthropologists (e.g., Simenel 2010) have argued that the status of integrated outsider or exile is the foundational position of Ichelhiyn Berber identity construction; a process not dissimilar to the idea of the Stranger-King as proposed by Sahlins (2008), albeit one not restricted to a particular elite group.

alterity which was understood to pervade social life more generally—one predicated on the notion that other people are, in some sense, unknowable per se. That they cannot be sounded or fathomed; their personality cannot be identified or used as a basis for prediction. This applies to everybody and it is this that is the fundamental hypothesis of mistrust: that, to reverse Simmel's maxim, there exists between our idea of a being and the being itself no definite connection or unity. As such, it is a stance that refuses psychological reductionism and embraces social and interactional complexity, rather than simplifying them for functional reasons. And it also refuses either to alienate or assert control. Trust may frequently be described as a way of managing the freedom of others, but, as we have seen, it is also a way of controlling it. Mistrust then, as we shall see, contributes rather to a philosophy of rugged autonomy and moral equality that assumes other people to be both free and fundamentally uncontrollable.

This book explores the origins and implications of this hypothesis, focusing on the core social assumptions of unknowability, irreducibility, and autonomy in a particular ethnographic site, that of the Moroccan High Atlas and using them as a basis for a broader analysis of the morphology of mistrust. In so doing, it also engages with and sometimes challenges a variety of scholarly and popular ideas about the role and nature of trust in society. At first blush, this might look like a derivative example of the sort of radical cultural comparison assayed by Marilyn Strathern in *The gender of the gift* (1988), where an idealized "System M" (for mistrust) is counterposed to a conventional portrayal of Western thought as represented by concepts of trust in the social sciences. It is not. For the simple reason that I do not see the two hypotheses I am describing as grounded in incompatible ontologies of, say, the person, society, or communication. To the contrary, they belong to the same conceptual universe. The ideas and practices that I describe as operative in the Moroccan High Atlas should be intuitively comprehensible to the reader, just as the sociological or linguistic theories I contrast them with are intuitively comprehensible to my friends in Morocco (when I explain them). The hypotheses of trust and mistrust are not mutually exclusive ways of viewing others, but are to an extent constitutive of one another. Each implies its shadow: where people assume that others can be known and so trusted, they are also aware that sometimes this does not hold; and where they assume that others are largely unknowable, they are also aware that some are less unknowable than others.

In short, this book is not an attempt to develop an opposition between two conceptual worlds. Instead, it pursues a wide range of different comparative strategies to further the twin aims of exploring the mistrust hypothesis in a particular context and challenging academic understandings of trust. I see these as fundamentally intertwined and mutually reinforcing processes, but also ones that are conceptually distinct and which, crucially, are not reducible to comparison.[15]

The first chapter explores the practical and conceptual bases of ideas of mistrust in the Moroccan High Atlas. As in certain other parts of the world, most notably Melanesia, local people claim that the inner worlds of others—their intentions, motivations, and character—are inscrutable and that the mere attempt to sound them is immoral. We can neither know nor faithfully represent the interiority of others to ourselves. This claim has radical implications for their ideas and practices of conversation and communication, as people both seek to shield their interiority from prying minds and refuse to speculate on that of others. This process of "lateral"[16] comparison between Melanesia and Morocco is used to expand standard pragmatic understandings of the form and function of speech. I suggest that in certain contexts and certain genres, lying or obfuscation is almost the default mode of speech and so the statements of others and even language itself are widely considered too labile to be trustworthy. Such lability is also a property of people themselves. As they are unknowable, they are also unpredictable and thus liable to betray one another.

The implications of these forms of mistrust for social relations, particularly friendship, are the subject of chapter 2. Here, I develop a frontal (and highly asymmetrical) comparison between classic *representations* of friendship in northwest Europe and actual *practices* of friendship in rural Morocco. Friendships are often the most relaxed, engaged, and intimate relations people have in the High Atlas, but they are not predicated upon a progressive unveiling of one's self to the other, nor are they built on foundations of trust. It is understood that friends may let you down or betray you. They are autonomous social actors and can neither be predicted nor bound, as trust requires. This, I argue, produces a much more tolerant and flexible form of friendship that allows for and

---

15. Except in the most banal possible acceptance of the term, whereby any act of exogenous description requires the juxtaposition (and thus comparison) of extraneous objects and concepts.

16. For a discussion of the differences between and implications of "lateral" comparison between different ethnographic objects and "frontal" comparison between an ethnographic object and the author's cultural hinterland, see Candea (2016).

accommodates fickleness and infidelity, and is based on affection and pleasure in one another's company rather than loyalty or identity.

This same flexibility is very much in evidence in local political practice, which I explore in chapter 3, comparing the High Atlas with other supposedly anarchist polities and using this directly to challenge some of the core assumptions of Western political theory. Standard representations of High Atlas politics, and indeed of Amazigh (Berber) politics more generally, focus on the village or tribal council as the locus of collective action. I paint a much more fluid picture of ephemeral institutions, unpredictable coalitions, and temporary constellations. This, I argue, is closer to traditional ethnographic representations of anarchy, with one key exception: where these latter tend to focus on the clear-sighted, idealistic nature of anarchic institutions, designed as bulwarks against tyranny, I propose to see them as a product of mistrust and oriented not to the ideal (or transcendent) but to the contingent (i.e. immanent).

The final chapter explores the variety of forms that mistrust can assume. It compares contemporary urban Ukraine with the Moroccan High Atlas, arguing that the very different infrastructures of everyday life characteristic of these two spaces allow for the proliferation of quite different imaginaries of mistrust. Places like Ukraine, or lowland Morocco, where the complex logistical frameworks of bureaucracy serve as the warp and weft of social existence, are fertile ground for conspiracy theories, which assume that organized subterranean forces are manipulating the contours of reality. In the more intimate and uncertain infrastructural environment of the High Atlas, meanwhile, different forms of mistrust flourish, centered around fears of the witch (the proximate enemy who betrays from within) and, above all, of the thief. A thief who targets objects, but also and especially a thief of information, who pries into your affairs, "steals your words," and compromises your autonomy.

CONTEXT AND CAVEAT

As must be clear, a great deal of the ensuing analysis draws on the two years I have spent living in the Moroccan High Atlas mountains with *Ishelhiyn* Berbers.[17] That said, I would like very seriously to stress that this book is not

---

17. It is currently fashionable to refer to all Berber-speaking people as Imazighen (sing. Amazigh or "free-man"), rather than the apparently pejorative word "Berber," which

primarily intended as an ethnography of a place or people; it is an ethnography of a hypothesis—that other human beings are irreducible and thus untrustworthy. My description and analysis of Atlassian life is, I trust, recognizable to those who actually live it, but it is also very partial—partial in that it focuses on the origins and implications of a *single* facet of existence. And even though the purpose of this book is in some sense to rescue mistrust from its universal pillory, it still involves depicting my friends as chronically suspicious and, insofar as it seeks to explain their suspicion, as frequent liars, occasional traitors, and opportunistic welchers. For most of my readers, these are not good things. And so, I would like to offer a pair of caveats. First, they are not good things for my friends in the Atlas either. Nobody likes being betrayed, lied to, or welched on, and nobody extols these things. Nor shall I. My purpose is not to say that mistrust is subjectively pleasant, but that some of the social effects of widespread mistrust are not necessarily corrosive, may at times even be enviable, and most importantly are worthy of sustained interest. And second, the people I lived and worked with are not reducible to their mistrust. They are also friends and lovers and doting parents; they are generous, unfailingly welcoming, and above all very fine company. I have not been able to do justice to these aspects of local life; that does not mean that they do not exist.

---

probably has the same root as barbarian. However, almost nobody I knew ever used the term in this sense. Instead, they referred to themselves as Ishelhiyn—i.e. people who speak Tashelhiyt, the largest of the three Moroccan Berber languages. The word Imazighen was reserved for the speakers of Tamazight, which is confusingly also the word for the specific Berber language spoken in the Middle Atlas region. I stick to local usage throughout.

CHAPTER I

Lying and obfuscation
The uncertain ground of speech

En vérité, le mentir est un maudit vice.	Lying, in truth, is an accursed vice.
Nous ne sommes hommes et ne nous tenons	We are only men and only cleave
les uns aux autres que par la parole	together by virtue of speech
	Montaigne

At the most basic level, speech and even language itself are predicated on a cer-tain minimal form of trust, also sometimes glossed as confidence.[1] We rely on the fact that the semantic field of a given word is more or less predictable over a limited time-frame. Without such predictability, even quite simple everyday actions rapidly become impossible: how to follow directions to the baker's if left and right are unstable terms? How to find an address? Ask for the salt? And if we cannot depend on words to mean what they mean, why communicate in the first place? This necessary semantic stability is, as Bakhtin (1981) argued, in part a simple by-product of interaction: by repeatedly using words within a community of speakers, we counteract their inherent centrifugal tendencies and

---

1. Luhmann (1988) argues that if one does not consider alternatives (e.g., when Europeans unthinkingly leave the house each morning unarmed), then one is in a situation of confidence, rather than trust, which implies risk. This distinction is not, however, universally followed and Luhmann himself insists on the close interrelatedness of the two concepts.

keep their meaning within recognizable bounds; and if the community splits up or does not use them often enough, they cease to be trustworthy and thus new languages are born and disused words break up like spindrift. Interaction alone, however, is not enough. We also rely on the goodwill of our fellow speakers insofar as we rely on them, as a rule, to use words in recognizable, systematic, and truthful ways.

What is true at this very basic level is also, *mutatis mutandis*, true of the more complex aspects of speech and communication, where this basic confidence also segues into slightly more extended forms of trust. For instance, as soon as one moves beyond utterly straightforward exchanges of information ("which bowl contains the salt?"), words cease to have any clear and stable transcontextual meaning. Instead, speakers and listeners have respectively to generate and infer meaning from context: think of the difference between "the house is on fire," "the basketball player is on fire [i.e., performing well]," and "that young fellow is on fire [i.e., attractive]." And in order for this transcontextual generation of meaning to be effective, we must once again trust that our interlocutors are working towards the same goal we are—viz. mutual comprehension.[2] We must assume that they are using words in ways that are intended to help us understand something about the situation or object to which they refer. This superficially simple insight is the central conceit of Grice's (1975) highly influential theory of conversational implicature, which explores the necessary contours of these mutual assumptions that underpin all acts of communication. Foremost among these, Grice suggests, is the default assumption that one's interlocutor is telling the truth. Once more, we must trust our interlocutors.

What, though, of situations where possible falsehood is so generalized within particular speech genres or with regard to specific subjects that such an assumption becomes untenable? Not for language as a whole, for this again would ultimately undermine the very possibility of its existence, but nonetheless for large swathes of everyday speech. What are the contours of communication in a place like the Moroccan High Atlas, where certain classes of statement are systematically presented and understood as inherently unreliable and the default listener position is thus one of mistrust? This chapter unpicks the social uses and abuses of these ambiguous genres, linking them to wider understandings of

---

2.   That this is closer to Luhmann's idea of trust than to confidence is testified to by the fact that we do sometimes ask ourselves whether our interlocutors are in fact working toward the same conversational ends as we are.

personhood, intimacy and social life. It also explores their impact on local understandings of the nature and purpose of language, as well as people's implicit ideas of discursive truth.

CONVERSATION AS COOPERATION

Grice's theory of implicature starts from the premise that conversation is at heart a cooperative endeavor. By this, he means that when we engage in any form of interactive speech, our comments are not (outside of late modernist theatre) "a succession of disconnected remarks" (1975: 45), but aim insofar as possible to work towards mutual understanding. He dubs this the "cooperative principle" and glosses it in the following terms: "make your conversational contribution such as is required, at the stage at which it occurs, by the accepted purpose or direction of the talk exchange in which you are engaged" (Grice 1975: 45). Under the umbrella of this overarching principle, he further identifies four specific maxims, with their relevant sub-maxims:

1. **Maxim of Quantity**
   a. Make your contribution as informative as is required (for the current purposes of the exchange)
   b. Do not make your contribution more informative than is required
2. **Maxim of Quality:** 'try to make your contribution one that is true'
   a. Do not say what you believe to be false
   b. Do not say that for which you lack evidence
3. **Maxim of Relation:** 'be relevant'
4. **Maxim of Manner:** 'be perspicuous'
   a. Avoid obscurity of expression
   b. Avoid ambiguity
   c. Be brief (avoid unnecessary prolixity)
   d. Be orderly   (1975: 45–6)

He then goes on to note that the first half of the maxim of quality ("do not say what you believe to be false") should be thought of as logically prior to the other three insofar as they are essentially nugatory unless the listener can assume that it has been fulfilled—i.e., unless we can suppose a statement to be true, it is little use asking whether it is sufficiently informative. At this point, it is important to stress that Grice is not suggesting that these maxims should be thought of either as guidelines for speech or as descriptions of what actually happens in conversation. He does not, in other words, contend that people either should or do follow them all or even most of the time. Rather, they are best thought of as the set of assumptions about other people's speech acts that it is reasonable to make, all other things being equal. The twist of course is in the tail, for all other things are rarely equal and Grice immediately proceeds to explore all the different ways in which the maxims may be broken: by "violation" such as lying (in which case the cooperative principle is in fact abandoned); by explicitly "opting out" ("I cannot say"); by virtue of a "clash" between two maxims; or by blatantly "flouting" one of them. It is this final case that particularly holds Grice's attention and which typically gives rise to conversational implicature, the idea being that if I openly flout a maxim, the listener is entitled to assume that I am doing so *in order* to make some further point—i.e., in the higher interests of communication.

Take, for instance, a situation where my sister asks me if our cousin's new husband is good-looking and I reply, "Well … he's well-built, nice curly hair, firm handshake, that sort of thing." Superficially, these seem like positive comments that suggest he is fairly handsome. But, they also clearly flout the maxim of quantity by giving far more information than was either required or requested and, on a secondary level, they also flout the maxim of relevance by mentioning his handshake in response to a question about looks. I could just have easily have responded "Yes" and then embellished the response afterwards. The fact that I chose not to do so and so flouted the maxims can thus be taken as intent to "implicate" something else—viz. that he is not in fact so handsome after all. In this example, the selective flouting of a particular maxim allows the speaker to indicate a dislocation between the surface meaning of a statement and its intended meaning, or what Grice respectively calls "timeless meaning" and "utterer's meaning" (1969).

It is this process of implicature, which is immediately recognizable to any speaker of a natural language, that primarily interests Grice, but outside of the field of linguistics, it is the maxims that have largely retained scholarly attention. And with good reason. Grice's claim is a bold one: that the maxims can be seen as universal baseline assumptions that it is reasonable to make in communicative interaction. Such grand, transversal claims have obvious cross-disciplinary appeal as a starting point for debate. Nowhere is this more true than in anthropology, which has made the debunking of putative universals something of a disciplinary specialty, which is why the relative lack of attention paid to the maxims from within the discipline is rather surprising. They do, after all, offer a framework for cross-cultural exploration of such eminently anthropological questions as how the relevance of chains of comments is differently construed in different sociocultural contexts or what is an acceptable level of conversational ambiguity. Their neglect is perhaps best understood as part of a wider disciplinary disdain for the pragmatic tradition (at least within mainstream Anglo-Saxon anthropology).[3]

Grice's theories have not, however, been entirely neglected within mainstream anthropology and what work there is has indeed been focused squarely on the maxims. As early as 1976, Keenan challenged the "universality of conversational postulates," notably suggesting that the maxim of quantity ("be informative") does not hold good in a Malagasy context. Whereas Grice contends that the maxim implies an expectation on the part of the hearer that her informational needs should be met, Keenan counters that Malagasy speakers have no such expectations. In the rural setting where her work appears to have been conducted, Keenan contends that most information is shared and "new information is a rare commodity" (1976: 70) that speakers guard closely. This is further compounded by a reluctance publicly to commit oneself to specific claims. Keenan concludes that whilst this does not entirely invalidate the maxim, it nonetheless mitigates it: "members of this speech community do not regularly expect that interlocutors will withhold necessary information. Rather, it is simply that they do not have the contrary expectation that, in general, interlocutors will satisfy one another's informational needs" (1976: 76). A very similar point is made quite independently by Dell Hymes, when he remarks in passing that "in a good many peasant societies, the foundation of prudent speech is to say no more than, and only as much as, is good for the *speaker*" (1983: xv, original emphasis).

In other words, both Keenan and Hymes accept the core architecture of Grice's theory of implicature, whilst insisting that the particular assumptions we make of our conversational partners admit of a degree of cultural variability. My argument here does not stray far from this template, but it focuses instead on the maxim of quality and on the social implications of this variability in conversational assumptions. In so doing, I draw on my own fieldwork in highland Morocco, as well as on two recent works by Senft (2008) and Danziger (2010)

---

3. Such disdain is largely absent from the field of linguistic anthropology (e.g., Duranti and Goodwin 1992) as well as from some other national traditions, notably in France, where both linguistic anthropology and the local incarnation of pragmatic sociology (e.g., Boltanski and Thévenot 1987; Dodier 1993) has had a strong influence on contemporary anthropology (e.g., Séveri and Bonhomme 2009).

that address similar issues, albeit reaching quite different conclusions, in the Trobriand Islands and among the Mopan Maya.

BERBER BULL

The most striking example of the liberties taken with the maxim of quality in the Moroccan High Atlas is perhaps in informal public or semi-public interaction. This, in my experience, is true for both male and female group sociality, although the more public and thus more superficially performative nature of interactions between men, as well as my more frequent and easier access to them, makes them the more obvious ethnographic object. As in many parts of the wider Mediterranean region, a good deal of male socializing is conducted in relatively large groups and in public places.[4] This is particularly so in winter, when the agricultural and pastoral cycles are at their least intensive and people to (especially male people) have plenty of time on their hands. Unless they have some particular errand to run or task to perform, most men do not leave the house until mid-morning, when they gradually begin to gather on the sunlit side of valleys or on the roofs of collective granaries to warm their cold bones and loosen their tongues. In larger villages, this normally means that they socialize with other men from their immediate neighborhood, who are also typically their extended kin, as villages are informally organized into agnatic districts. They then return to their houses for lunch and only re-emerge in mid-afternoon, when they either make their way to their mosque or to the entrance to the village where shops and, more recently, cafés are located. This time, the groups are often somewhat larger (up to fifteen or twenty men) and more diverse, as anybody is in principle welcome to take a seat, although in practice there is a certain degree of clustering by age and inclination. Sometimes, people engage in minor agricultural tasks such as shelling walnuts or peeling iris roots, but most men are simply there to talk and this talk takes particular forms.

Much of it is given over to the exchange of general information—prices at the market, the weather, local events or, for younger villagers, football

---

4.   See Gilsenan's *Lords of the Lebanese marches* (1996) for a total portrait of male sociability in the rural Middle East. He notably explores the dynamics of speech and performance in a variety of public and semi-public group settings, such as *saḥarāt* (similar to *zzewerda*—see below), where men gather to tell stories, play cards, jostle for status, and engage in competitive humor.

results—but a goodly part of the rest is devoted to idle chatter. This rarely involves personal gossip, which men tend to shun as a public genre, though they are frequently extremely partial to it in more private settings. Instead, it has a loose and slightly desultory quality, characterized by something like *esprit*, or what local people, if pressed for a term, call *awal ifulkin* (beautiful talk). This sometimes espouses the contours of recognized narrative genres (riddles, jokes, stories, and anecdotes—each of which has its own conventions), but mostly it involves either agonistic forms of teasing and verbal jousting or, alternatively, the collaborative construction of light-hearted conversation. In my experience, none of these different forms (narrative, agonistic or collaborative) has much truck with the truth. Rather, they all to a greater or lesser degree, strive to inhabit a space of unverifiable possibility. In other words, they recount things that *might just* be true. This is very evident in the tales people tell, but also in the more agonistic forms of interaction, especially those involving semi-outsiders such as anthropologists whose ingenuousness radically expands the scope of possibility. Let me give a pair of examples:

On gesticulation

Some four or five months after my arrival in the field, I was gathered with a group of twenty or so men in the entrance to the village. Conversation had turned, as it periodically did, to me, and my interlocutors were taking turns to ask vaguely prurient or ambiguous questions that I would be either embarrassed or unable to answer. Much laughter ensued and I bore my baiting with practiced stoicism, struggling to respond in a combination of halting and stammered Tashelhiyt and plenty of compensatory hand-gestures. Suddenly, a man called 'Abdullah, whose normal diction was a slightly hysterical falsetto, adopted a sterner tone and cut across the medley of mellow voices: "You shouldn't wave your hands about like that! We are mountain people. We don't get all excited like that. We keep our hands in our lap when we talk." "Really? (*Ima'qul?*)" *I asked.* "Really!" *The conversation then broke up into smaller units and a multitude of directions until some five minutes later, the man sat to my left whispered,* "Ask 'Abdullah what the word 'horse' means." "A 'Abdullah! Ma igan ayyis?" *I duly enquired. 'Abdullah looked up at me and made the universal Tashelhiyt sign for horse: index and middle finger bouncing up and down as the hand moves sideways. Everybody laughed.*

The second example took place in a third major setting of semi-public sociality, the evening dinner party (*zzerda*),[5] which is normally held late at night on winter evenings. Groups of men, often relatively coeval friends or acquaintances, meet up in an empty house somewhere in the village around nine in the evening, after they have eaten their standard evening meal of barley or maize couscous at home. One of them brings a cockerel, which they slaughter and cook in a tagine with whatever vegetables are to hand. This takes two to three hours and in the meantime, they drink tea, play cards, and talk. After they have eaten, they have one last cup of tea, settle up for the cockerel, and then the party swiftly breaks up and they make their way home, warning one another to be on guard against thieves and marauders (see chapter 4). When I had lived in the village, such parties often took place at my house, as the absence of women and children meant that it counted as empty for the sake of partying, but on this occasion, it was in an abandoned house in the center of the village. I had been brought along against the wishes of some of the younger members of the party who justifiably feared that my inability to play a full part in the linguistic play characteristic of such gatherings would put a damper on the festivities. The atmosphere was accordingly a little tense and one of the young men, Idir, adopted a slightly brash, pugnacious, and entertaining persona that, though common in the plains, sat uneasily with the less aggressive interactive styles typical in a mountain setting:

On shepherds

The conversation had turned, after some havering, to sex. I had suggested, as conversational bait, that it might be in somewhat short supply in Morocco and had degraded myself in a culturally inappropriate way by putting forward my own long-enforced chastity as evidence of this. I then gestured in a friendly way towards Idir and said "What about you? You haven't got a wife." *Idir sat up and laughed, before insisting that despite being unmarried, he still got plenty.* "I," *he said,* "am a shepherd (*amksa*)"—"Ah," *I replied,* "and God has provided sheep in plenty?"—"No," *he laughed a little awkwardly,* "you don't know what a

---

5.   See Hoffman (2007) for a comparative perspective on mixed-gender *zzewerda* in the Moroccan Anti-Atlas, where the emphasis is apparently more on groups of young people playing music, singing and dancing together (60–72). In the area where I worked, this would have been considered extremely licentious and totally unacceptable.

shepherd is. When men are out working the fields, who has free time (*ma isallan*)? When women are up in the high mountains for summer, who has free time? Shepherds. I am a shepherd. And not just once either.*"—"Really?" (lma'qul) I said—"Really!"*

Before continuing, I should stress that though the scope of such playful talk is expanded by the naivety and ignorance of the anthropologist or other semi-outsiders, the style is not reserved for such people and is in fact restricted to nominally intra-group relations—complete strangers will not, for reasons of propriety, be included in such exchanges. Indeed, this form of teasing is also used as a tool of integration, as in the first example when I was "fed lines" so I could defend myself (cf. de Vienne 2012), as well of course so they could use me as a proxy soldier in internal battles. It is also interesting to note that unlike in similar such contexts discussed elsewhere in the Mediterranean (cf. Gilsenan 1976), the point here does not seem to be to hoodwink the listener in order to then ridicule him for his gullibility, but instead to deepen and dwell in the ambiguity they generate. And therein lies the crux. For what is really striking about these examples is that ten years and twenty months of fieldwork later, much of the ambiguity is still there: I am still largely unable to assess the truth value of some of the statements made.

I can say that Tashelhiyt interactional styles in mountain areas (especially in the Central High Atlas where I worked) are notably more sober than in the plains. People are more composed, more reserved, less excitable and more puritanical. They probably do wave their hands about a bit less. I can also say, with near certainty, that a great deal of philandering goes on in the village where I lived. What I cannot say is whether 'Abdullah really meant to convey that gesticulatory sobriety was an explicit social norm, and no more can I say whether Idir really meant me (and the others) to believe that he was, in the village context, a recidivist "shepherd." This, as I have said, is because the speech genres deployed in these contexts are non-committal with regard to the truth. What this means is not only that I cannot make any assumptions about their status, but also that they are excessively hard to verify with other people. So, I waited until the dinner party had ended and asked the close friend who had brought me along whether he thought Idir was a "shepherd," but his reply was not "yes," "no," or "maybe," nor even "who knows?" Instead, he simply negated the question by responding "*Ghayr wawal a iga*" (it's just words/speech). This phrase can be a way of drawing a contrast between speech and action (as in the English locution, "he's all talk"), but it is also, as it was here, a direct reflection on the status of speech. The question of its truth is neither here nor there. This does not, of course, prevent my friend from having an opinion about whether or not Idir is a shepherd; it simply means that Idir's claims in this particular context are not really seen as having any bearing on the question. The same was true of 'Abdullah's assertion of Tashelhiyt gestural sobriety; my subsequent queries as to whether this was true were met with only laughter and perhaps slight bafflement at the stupidity of the question.

In this, the situation is in some ways very comparable to that described by Senft in the Trobriand Islands. Senft argues that Kilivila (the local language) is divided into eight recognizable speech genres, including "magic language" (*biga megwa*), "church language" (*biga tapwaroro*), and "heavy" or "direct language" (*biga mokwita*). The most common of these genres and the default form of Trobriand speech is, however, *biga sopa* (joking or lying language).[6] This genre encompasses joking, story-telling, gossip and so forth and it is "marked by features that include 'vagueness' or 'ambiguity'" (2008: 141). What is more, *biga sopa*, like informal Tashelhiyt public speech, is characterized by the speaker's "unmarked non-commitment to the truth" (Hanks, pers. comm. in *ibid.*). As such, both *biga sopa* and Tashelhiyt public speech pose something of a problem for Grice's theory of implicature, for what we have is whole speech genres predicated on the systematic transgression of the maxim of quality with no compensatory payoff in terms of meaning. Because it is unmarked, the failure to conform to the maxim is not used to generate a semantic surplus that can be used to direct the listener's process of inference; it is not flouted in the higher interests of communicational cooperation. Rather, it is just part and parcel of the genre.

This leads Senft to contend that because *biga sopa* is the default speech genre, "'truth' is in general an irrelevant quality or feature of … everyday conversation and discourse" (2008: 142), and the maxim of quality is also therefore irrelevant to the local context. Drawing on earlier work suggesting that this same maxim

---

6. See Stewart (1989) for a related discussion of the distinction between everyday, and slightly untrustworthy, speech (*duma*) and "true speech" (*caco vorba*) among Hungarian Vlax Roma. This distinction is taken up by Foisneau (2016), who argues that significant parts of everyday speech among so-called Hungarian Roma in France is characterized by a very loose relationship to the truth. She refers to this genre as "true-lying" (*vrai-mensonge*), in perhaps implicit homage to Aragon's *Le mentir-vrai* (1980).

of quality is also irrelevant to ritual communication (Wheelock 1982; Haiman 1998), Senft proceeds to conclude that *biga sopa* is also a form of ritual communication and one that in classical Durkheimian fashion "serves the functions of social bonding and of blocking aggression" (2008: 142). Basically, he argues, speech is not about communication, but about reinforcing communal ties. And it is here that our analytical paths separate. For whilst I agree with him—and incidentally with Malinowski (1935), Austin (1962), and everybody else—that speech is not merely about communication, I have a hard time admitting that truth in general, and the assumption of truthfulness, can be "irrelevant" to the majority of everyday speech. It is hard to see how language would survive this. It is, in any event, certainly not a fair description of what is going on in the High Atlas case outlined above, as the speech genre in question is, in fact, fairly limited in scope, both in terms of context and content. As we have seen, it is typically restricted to public or semi-public performance and, just as importantly, the license it takes with the truth does not embrace the gamut of representational possibilities. Its speakers do not just invent things willy-nilly; the whole point of such speech is precisely its plausibility. In other words, everything should be true except for the essential narrative content or point and, as such, it does not sap the fundaments of conversation and communication and it does not entirely sidestep the maxim of quality.

What it suggests, more than anything, is that Grice, and to a lesser extent his successors such as Levinson (2000), take too narrow a view of conversation as essentially concerned with the transmission of useful information about the world. For Grice, the maxim of quality can only be flouted if it allows the speaker to convey additional information, whereas in the cases I have described, the maxim is transgressed in the interests of entertainment.[7] This, though, should be seen more as an addition than as a direct challenge to the theory. Grice would not, I suspect, have suggested that all speech genres are principally concerned with the communication of useful information: poetry and song, for instance, are not necessarily supposed to be true. Their purpose is more commonly to amuse, beguile, or entertain, and this can also be true of conversation. All we need to do is suggest that conversational maxims can be flouted both in order to allow the speaker to implicate something extra or to generate additional

---

7. This, of course, is a fairly broad category and we might equally speak of conviviality, cruelty, or laughter as significant conversational ends. It would be interesting to explore these finer distinctions in greater depth.

amusement.[8] And we do not need to go all the way to the Trobriands or the Moroccan High Atlas to find such conversational genres; the "bull-sessions" discussed by Frankfurt (1986) or the "shit-talking" apparently practiced in some African-American communities (Abrahams 1964; cf. Laudun 2012), in which people engage in the fictional elaboration of a real-world theme (e.g., that time we found the treasure in the backwoods) would fit the bill just as well.

A much more serious challenge to the theory is, however, posed by other floutings of the maxim of quality in the Moroccan High Atlas—ones that display far more flexibility in terms of context and scope.

PLAUSIBLE, POSSIBLE FALSEHOODS

If you meet a man on one of the paths that lead to or from your village, you should stop, wish him peace, inquire after his health and condition, and then either ask him where he's going or where he's coming from. Sometimes, especially if he suspects that you already know where he's been (in which case the question is still appropriate), he may give you a straight answer; more likely, he will obfuscate or otherwise parry the question ("I'm just wandering around"); and sometimes often he will shrug his shoulders, perhaps crack a broad smile or adopt a slightly sing-song voice and offer a plausible response. The status of such responses is exquisitely hard to assess. The listener should not assume them to be true, but no more are they necessarily false and even when they *are* false, they are often apparently pointlessly so.

People may say that they have been herding their sheep when they were actually visiting their sister, or that they went to market to buy tomatoes, when in fact they shod their mule (in which case the follow-up question should be what the going price for tomatoes was so you can triple-check it with other market-goers). It does not really matter what response is given so long as it's plausible and, above all, it does not really matter whether your interlocutor believes you, because you have in any case meta-pragmatically distanced yourself from the statement with the shrugging and smiling. Here, as in the speech-genres described above, the purpose of such floutings of the maxim of quality is

---

8.   It is also worth noting that amusement or entertainment are ends that, unlike Senft's Durkheimian idea of reinforcing social bonds, are not methodologically collectivist (cf. Paine 1967). This, I maintain, makes them a little more credible.

not to fool the other person, but to generate uncertainty, muddy the waters, and thicken the epistemological fog; unlike, however, in informal Tashelhiyt public speech (and perhaps in Trobriand *biga sopa*), it does not do so for purposes of entertainment. It is not, after all, so very funny to tell people that you bought carrots not potatoes at market or that you were irrigating in Ayt Fulan, when in fact you were ferrying manure to Imi n Talat.

Nor is it a genre restricted to specific social contexts; to the contrary, people engage in this sort of low-level and attritional mendacity—which I have elsewhere described as a form of lying from which the intention to deceive is absent[9]—in all sorts of situations and with all sorts of people. I recall one conversation with my "field sister": I had just visited her brother in Marrakesh, where he was working for a pittance in an upmarket pizzeria near the central square in the old town. She asked me if I knew how much he earned, because at the time he was remitting virtually nothing to the family, who were struggling financially. I said that I didn't know, and asked why she hadn't posed the question to him when he was back home for *'ayd* a month or two ago. She had, she said, "*but of course he lied to me: I'm his sister.*" This statement is worth underlining as it underscores the idea raised in the introduction that mistrust reaches right into the heart of relations of kinship.

Where it does perhaps admit of restrictions is in terms of the content of such possible falsehoods. If a friend explains to me how to butcher a sheep, perform prayer, plough a field, bury a son, or shoe an ass, then I do not expect him to lie. If she draws me a map of the tribal sub-fraction, explains about the history of the village, or tells me the names of the different trees, then Grice's maxim of quality still largely holds good. Even gossip about other people is still essentially subject to an expectation of truthfulness: though I may recognize that gossip is inherently untrustworthy (*ibergagn ur shin*—tittle-tattle is unreliable), it does not follow that I suppose my interlocutor to be in bad faith when he recounts it to me. But such expectations are, I suggest, no longer typically present when it comes to personal information—when a friend tells me which Qur'anic school he studied in, how many years he lived outside the village, etc. In some cases the speaker may play it rather straight and in others he may go so far as to openly declare that he is "lying," but in almost all of them his words are subject to doubt. In other words, such possible falsehoods traverse speech genres, but are restricted in two other ways. First, along lines of gender. Unlike the

---

9.   "Ce que mentir veut dire" (unpublished manuscript).

previous genre of semi-public speech, this sort of mistruth is, I think, more the domain of men than women. Certainly women practice the same sort of quotidian obfuscation as men when asked about their whereabouts or movements, but they are, in my experience, more likely to provide a seemingly straight answer when questioned about other personal issues (such as property, kinship relations, or opinions). And second, it is restricted in terms of content: such statements concern the speaker.

Interestingly, there is precedent for discussions of this sort of untruth, or rather "a-truth" in Moroccanist anthropology. Lawrence Rosen argues, in *The anthropology of justice* (1989), that statements made by Moroccans in the process of establishing relationships are best understood as "negotiating positions" that bear no actual relation to the truth (1989: 184). Rather than serving to transmit information about the speaker, they help him or her to achieve particular social ends—in this case, the establishment of new social ties. So, when two men meet in a market context, they will discuss themselves, their origins and profession in a non-committal way so as to maximize the possibility of finding some point of overlap that will allow them to drive the relationship forward. This, though, is slightly different to what I am describing, because it is clearly restricted to a particular social setting: the establishing of new relations. As such, we can see it as another variation on the idea outlined above: that speech may serve purposes other than communication—social integration, amusement, or relationship-building—in which case the maxim of quality can be flouted in their higher interest. The type of speech under discussion here is, in contrast, far more generalized across contexts, is (in my experience and that of my Ishelhiyn interlocutors) vastly more present in the mountains than in the plains, and cannot be seen as subjugated to any mutually recognized conversational goal. In order, then, to understand what is at stake here, we need to take a brief digression through local ideas of personhood and, in particular, the striking notion that the inner worlds of others are basically impervious to scrutiny.

THE HERMENEUTIC VEIL

This idea, that in some parts of the world other people's psychic and emotional interiority is held to be fundamentally inscrutable, is by now a well-established one within anthropology. In 2008, Joel Robbins and Josh Rumsey edited a special edition of the *Anthropological Quarterly* exploring what they called "the opacity of other's minds." These articles largely focused on the insular Pacific[10] and trained their gaze most particularly on questions of how local ideologies of opacity run up against practices of Christian confession (Keane 2008; Robbins 2008), although they also explored questions of autonomy (Stasch 2008) and gossip (Schieffelin 2008) that are of central interest to us here. The authors stressed that the idea was not a new one in a Melanesian context and we can, for instance, find very similar claims in some of the earlier work of Strathern where she remarks that "people [in Hagen] regard themselves as chronically unable to read off the intentions of others" (1985: 127); and if we stretch our field to Polynesia, then Margaret Mead noted as early as 1928 that Samoans show an "odd incuriousness about motive" (1928: 123). It is only, however, over the last several years that it has become a recognizable lemma of anthropological thought and at the time I was conducting my principal fieldwork, from 2003 to 2005, it scarcely registered on the wider disciplinary radar.

As such, it was not something that I initially focused on during my research and, perhaps surprisingly, it was also something that it took me an inordinately long time—in fact well over a year—to notice. One of the appealing things about traditional immersion fieldwork is that the anthropologist ideally acquires a language and a way of life at roughly the same rhythm, such that the two may appear seamlessly to elide into one another. This perhaps explains the disciplinary appeal of linguistic relativism; it also generates particular cultural blind spots in the researcher.

In my case, these concerned the remarkable absence of explanations by character or intention. I quite simply failed to notice that people scarcely ever attributed durable personality traits either to themselves or others, and because I had learned the language *in situ*, it had not really occurred to me to do so either. Until, that is, one evening shortly before I left the field when I was out walking with two good friends and one remarked, in passing, that a mutual acquaintance had "tamkhamakht *in him*"—"*And what,*" I duly inquired, "*is tamkhamakht?,*" only for my friend to patiently explain the concept of vanity, before pulling up short and saying, "*But of course, we are all a little vain. I'm vain; you're vain. And so he's a bit vain. Not much, just a bit.*" And as he did so, it struck me that whilst I knew plenty of words for passing emotional states such as anger, envy, boredom, or sorrow (ones that can be read on the skin), and a handful of terms

---

10. Although similar phenomena have since been discussed in Inner Asia (e.g., da Col 2012), and Amazonia (Allard 2010; Walker 2015).

for easily observable behavioral traits (e.g., laziness—*tamkhaynt*), I lacked a whole vocabulary for describing people's character. I would later find out that such terms do of course exist, though they are frankly fairly limited in scope and number, and are a frequent topic of poetry and song, where they can be discussed in the abstract.[11] They are, however, very rarely applied to people. This struck me as interesting, but nothing more, and I filed it away for future reference.

It was only when I returned to Europe a few months later and was once again immersed in a social environment predicated upon the ceaseless interrogation of other people's inner worlds and the subsequent imputation to them of psychological states, that I realized how comparatively strange this in fact was. In the United Kingdom, and in the upper-middle-class context of university life (as opposed to the partially working-class context of my upbringing), any social gathering will likely be followed by a "post-mortem" among intimates, during which the personalities of those present will be dissected, partly for pleasure and partly so as to keep one's hand in. People seemed constantly to be engaged in describing *how* other people were, and when they gossiped, the recounting of supposed acts, arguments, or indiscretions seemed little more than a prelude to the serious business of wondering *why* the people involved had behaved the way they did. [We don't really care that Mary cheated on Bill; we want to speculate about why she did so. After all, Bill's so nice; perhaps she's unhappy in her job; or maybe she wants to destroy her relationship to prove to herself how fundamentally unlovable she is].[12] This too, I realized, was something that had been quite absent from my seventeen months in Morocco. Gossip (*ibergagn*), as in any society, and especially small-scale rural ones, is a staple part of daily life; and as an anthropologist, for whom gossip is essentially what passes for data, I had played as full a role in this as my limited means allowed. Yet I could scarcely remember a situation in which the gossip had extended to an exploration of people's motives or intentions and, I noticed in retrospect, my periodic queries as to why people had behaved the way they did had been given systematically short shrift: *ma isen?* (who knows?) *ghayr mkand* (that's just how it is); *mkada tga* (that's how she is). In other words, they strive heroically to avoid the fundamental attribution error: the well-recognized tendency to explain a person's behavior in terms of internal psychological characteristics rather than the external factors

---

11. See, for instance, El Mountassir's *Amarg: chants et poésies amazighs* (2004), which features for instance a poem explicitly dedicated to the theme of *lkibr* (pride).

12. Freud, in short, has won the battle for the hearts and minds of Western civilization.

of a situation. They refuse, to return to an idea mentioned in the introduction, to functionally simplify reality by appealing to a synthetic concept of personality (Luhmann 1979: 41).

When I returned to the field in 2008 for a postdoctoral project, it was with this idea, rather than my official research on conceptions of illness, that I principally tormented my friends and interlocutors. To a man (and a woman), they confirmed it. Other people's inner worlds were inaccessible. One could not know their motives or intentions. One could not make durable claims about their character.[13] Not even the curmudgeonly shop-keeper, 'Abdullah, who had been grumpy every day for the last ten years; there were no legitimate grounds for supposing he might still be so tomorrow. We could not divine what made him grumpy and so we could not augur its recurrence. People's inner selves were categorically unknowable and, somewhat paradoxically, it was immoral even to attempt to sound them. In the words of one female informant, others' inner worlds had been "veiled by god" (*isntl-tn rbbi*) and to attempt to penetrate the shroud was a fundamental act of trespass on their personal independence, what I shall henceforth describe as their *autonomy*.[14]

This notion, that other people are shrouded in a moral and epistemological *hermeneutic veil* is, I think, one that is central to social life and cultural repertoires in the area. It extends, as I have argued elsewhere (Carey 2010) not only to people, but also to non-human spirits (*djinn*) and even conditions people's understandings of the knowability of some natural phenomena, such as illnesses, whose origins and nature are widely considered impervious to human scrutiny—although the actual efficacy of medicine is not in doubt. It also gives rise to a radical respect for the moral and psychological autonomy of others (the ramifications of which we shall explore over the next two chapters); as Webb Keane notes for the Korowai of Papua New Guinea, "denying a universal human propensity for intention-seeking ... draws attention to and conceptually elaborates certain familiar experiences of inner thought, interactive miscues,

---

13. I should relativize this by noting that people, and especially younger people who grew up with the television, do occasionally say things like, "X often behaves in such and such a way because it's his nature (*tabi'a*) to do so." What they don't do is specify what this "nature" might actually be like.

14. It is not my purpose here to engage with the extensive literature on the origins and development of the idea of autonomy. I use it to render the highly prevalent local idea of a person's right to "do what his own head dictates" (*iskr win ikhfns*), and to do so free from the prying and intrusion of others.

secrecy, and deception. It brings these ubiquitous experiences to bear on quite particular ethical and political problems" (2017: 96). In the High Atlas, those ethical problems concern questions of autonomy. And perhaps most significantly for our purposes here, it shapes and constrains the contours of communication and conversation.

This assertion needs a caveat. I fully concur with authors such as Keane (2017) and Stasch (2008) in maintaining that it is unequivocally not the case that this public moratorium on psychological speculation equates to a lack of implicit reflection on or awareness of people's motives or intentions. Inhabitants of the High Atlas have a theory of mind—i.e., the capacity and tendency to attribute mental states to themselves and others (Premack and Woodruff 1978)—just like everybody else. As suggested above, it is quite impossible to interpret the meaning of even quite simple sentences unless we in some way impute intention to the speaker: when one's mother says "I wouldn't eat that biscuit if I were you," one must read her intentions in order to understand that it is a threat and not a statement; or when an angry Ashelhiy repeatedly punctuates his list of grievances with the query "*izd mkand?*" (is that how it is), it requires a theory of mind to know that one shouldn't answer.[15] Nor could complex forms of social life be sustained without sophisticated awareness of motive and, to a lesser extent, character, as well as the equally crucial capacity to communicate this awareness to other social actors—it is not, for instance, really credible to think about human society without the possibility of warnings or recommendations regarding other people. So the moratorium does not prevent speculation about mental states and nor can it entirely impede communication of such speculation, but it can and does radically constrain the ways in which people can discuss (and perhaps to a certain extent conceptualize) these things. In short, they need to find ways of evoking interiority and intention without appearing to do so.

The most straightforward way to do this is to treat visible behavior or actions as a shorthand or proxy for motive,[16] character, or intentions, to speak of

---

15. The question of how important intention actually is for understanding speaker-meaning is, in fact, vastly complicated (see Duranti 2015, for an overview), but as Duranti, himself a partial anti-intentionalist, states: "some kind of mind-reading obviously goes on in Samoa, as in any other place in the Pacific or elsewhere in the world" (2015: 235).

16. In the psychological literature, it is often argued that in low-information contexts, people "satisfice" (or make do with less than optimal strategy) by relying on ascriptive characteristics (i.e., personality traits) as a proxy for more complete information

them as if action and intention or mental state are fused. To give an example, on my most recent trip to the area, in May 2016, a good friend and I dropped by the house of a mutual acquaintance, Samir, from the plains who had moved from Tiflilist to a different village a few years back. My friend only stayed for half an hour, whereas I spent the night and most of the next day there. A week or so later, I ran into him back in Tiflilist and he asked how Samir was doing. I replied that I wasn't sure, but that I felt he had spent a very long time living in the mountains (*im'adl g udrar*). My friend replied, "*Yes, he has, have you seen how slatternly* (abkhulliy) *he's become*," referring to the squalor of his living arrangements, which was extreme even by fairly relaxed local standards. "*He used not to be like that*," I concurred. "*He's let his stubble grow*," added my friend. "*Perhaps he's not in such a good way. He'd do well to marry*." In this exchange, as I understood it, I basically suggested that Samir was lonely, and my friend replied that he was probably depressed and that this depression had been growing worse over the years. We both did so without explicitly referring to Samir's mental state or interiority, instead using elements of his observable behavior (distance from kin, squalid domestic situation, and stubble) as a proxy language for evoking them.

Once more, there is precedent for this in the pages of Lawrence Rosen's *The anthropology of justice*. Rosen notes that Moroccan judges claim to be able to "read rather directly from a person's words and deeds the intent that lies within" (1989: 51). Of course, for my interlocutors in the High Atlas, this sort of statement would be nothing short of anathema, but it may be that a similar underlying principle is at work: actions are seen as standing for intentions. It is also in some ways comparable to the Mayan case described by Danziger (2010) in her recent critique of precisely the same Gricean maxim of quality that interests us here. Danziger notably contends that speakers of Mopan Maya typically do not distinguish between deliberate lies and accidental falsehoods in their moral judgments. It is not the *intent* to lie that is blameworthy, but the *fact* of having misled the other—the gravity of which is then assessed in terms of damage done (2010: 204).[17] She argues that this shows that the reading of intention is not necessarily integral to communication, but one might also contend that

---

(cf. Cook 2001: xvii). What I am describing here can be seen as an even more radical form of satisficing in which ascriptive characteristics are replaced by actions.

17.   Interestingly, Mopans also agree with Thomas Aquinas that fiction should be seen as a form of lie (*Summa theologica*, second part of the second part, question 110).

people are simply avoiding the public imputation of intention (the Tashelhiyt term for lies, *ikirkisn*, similarly covers both falsehoods and lies).[18] In any case, I suggest that this fusion of action and intention means that when people in the Moroccan High Atlas gossip, as they so frequently do, they use the very detailed discussion of people's behavior as a means of implicitly reflecting on and communicating elements of intention and character. And this is morally extremely problematic, as it constitutes an implicit breach of other people's right to psychic autonomy.

If this is so, then it perhaps helps explain men's aversion to public gossip; for it is not that they do not enjoy it in private; and it is not that a detailed interest in the private lives of others is considered feminine or unmanly *per se* (as might be the case in some European societies).[19] There is, of course, the universal problem of not making unnecessary problems for oneself by being seen to slander the friends or intimates of one's audience, but much gossip in mountain areas concerns outsiders such as teachers who often have neither friends nor intimates. Yet even in such cases, it would be unseemly to discuss their shenanigans in a public arena. Perhaps one reason why this is so is the broad-based attachment to a scrupulous moral egalitarianism (between free Ishelhiyn men,[20] I hasten to add) in the High Atlas region—one which involves not only refusing publicly to be coerced, but just as importantly, avoiding being seen to coerce others.[21] To strong-arm is egregious; to impinge on others repugnant (Carey 2007). And if gossip is a shorthand for discussion of intention and interiority, and discussion of interiority is trespass on the autonomy of others, then gossip

---

18. On a related note, there is also Michelle Rosaldo's extraordinary anecdote of an Ilongot man who dropped his load of game on a gun, thereby causing it to fire and kill him. This was interpreted as punishment for his nephew's breaking of an oath of peace, but actual culpability was not assigned to the nephew; instead, the owner of the gun was identified as morally responsible (1982: 219–20). Here, intention has been entirely removed from the frame in favor of a focus on the moral identification of objects and people.

19. For a discussion of the roots of European attitudes towards gossip and gender in late classical antiquity and the New Testament, see Kartzow (2009), which explores the frequent correlation (and condemnation) of notions of idleness, domesticity, gossip, and womanhood.

20. Thus excluding women, former slaves, and descendants of blacksmiths, who essentially belong to a different caste in traditional southern Morocco.

21. See Stasch (2008) for a comparable argument about the relationship between an ideology of opacity and egalitarianism.

is *ipso facto* an impingement on the independence of others.[22] It will not do to be seen publicly to gossip.

More importantly still, this three-way association of gossip about the actions of others, implicit appraisal of their intentions and trespass on their autonomy allows us to return to the original question of what is at stake when people engage in the sort of plausible falsehoods described above, making statements that cannot be labeled as either true or false. They are clearly not seeking to fool anybody, or they would lie better, without all the meta-pragmatic indicators of non-commitment like shrugging and smiling and altering their tone. Instead, I suggest, the purpose of such apparently pointless lies is simply *to prevent one's interlocutor from being sure of the truth*, whatever that may be. In so doing, people preserve a space of psychic and moral autonomy by shrouding their actions in mystery. On a side note, this also helps explain why women seem to utter such lies a little less often: they may be keen to hide their movements for reasons of privacy, safety, shame, and so on, but their public identities are less tied up with questions of autonomy, which in its literal sense of self-determination is discursively denied them and whose moral and psychic extensions are accordingly less fraught. To be clear, I am not suggesting that there is a straightforward causal relationship between the idea of a hermeneutic veil and these linguistic strategies, but I do think that they clearly partake of the same epistemological construct. Now, in the final section, we return to the question of implications of this construct for wider attitudes toward language, truth, and people.

SUSPENDED VERACITY

As we saw above, certain speech genres—such as *biga sopa* in the Trobriand Islands or informal male public speech in the High Atlas—allow for Grice's maxim of quality, with its attendant default assumption of truthfulness, to be violated for the sake of amusement or entertainment. How, though, does the more attritional form of "lying" discussed above, one that traverses speech genres, affect this assumption? For Rosen (like Senft), these sorts of statements

---

22. See also Schieffelin (2008), who notes that gossip among the Bosavi of Papua New Guinea equates to "say[ing] something you do not have a right to say" and links it to questions of "ownership" of "unexpressed or inarticulate thoughts or desires" (2008: 434).

must be seen as pure performatives and have no truth-value for either speaker or listener. My point is slightly different. The truth or falsehood of many of these statements does matter, for both parties. It matters because in a world where you can't discuss intention, actions are all there is to go on. At the moment such statements are made, however, there is simply no way in which their truth-value can be assessed. Accordingly, listeners simply place them in inverted commas and wait until such time as reality, or more commonly third-party narratives, confirm or infirm them. We might, perhaps a little fancifully, call this a quantum theory of truth: the idea is that just as quantum particles in the Copenhagen interpretation are supposed to have no determinate values until they are measured, so people's utterances have no truth-value as such until they are tested: they exist in a state of suspended veracity. To be clear, unlike particle physicists and some recent anthropologists (e.g., Holbraad 2012), I am not making any ontological claim about the actual nature of truth. My point is purely heuristic: such statements *might as well* have no truth-value until put to proof and are treated accordingly.

This has two further implications. First, that people explicitly mistrust language as a tool of communication. They see it less as providing clarity and insight and more as generating ambiguity and throwing up a smokescreen. And second, that they mistrust one another. Other people are unknowable and their statements are not reliable guides to their actions or selves. Let me give one final example of this. I am in the habit, when I come up with some far-fetched interpretation of a particular aspect of High Atlas life, of waiting until next I visit the region and running it by some of my friends. The village where I have worked may be extremely remote by Moroccan standards, but it is not a stagnant intellectual backwater. Rather, it has a long history of sending men to the plains to study in Qur'anic schools for several years; this was practically a rite of passage for the men of the most prominent extended family, the Ayt Hassou, and as a result there are a large number of people familiar with the structure of complex theological, and therefore academic, debate.

In this particular case, I had been idly asking a group of friends what they thought about the primacy of aural metaphors in Tashelhiyt (as opposed to Arabic and many European languages). So people talk about "hearing" the sun on their skin (*slgh tadfi n tafuqt f tagullimt*) and tend to use aural rather than visual verbs in contexts related to understanding: "Do you hear?" rather than "Do you see?" One friend responded, in fine Pythagorean style, that this was because all external stimuli were in fact forms of vibration that were processed as sound—so the sun caused his skin to resonate and he perceived ("heard") this resonance as a form of pleasant heat. But nobody else had any very interesting ideas. Two weeks later, though, there was a knock on my door at eleven o'clock at night; it turned out to be 'Ali (see chapter 2). He sat down and explained that he had been thinking about my question and it seemed to him that it was related to the manner of accessing the truth. The Arabs had a centuries-old tradition of accessing the truth about reality (*lḥaqq*) in written form, via the Qur'an and other texts; most Ichelhiyn, in contrast, were illiterate—their access to reality was mediated through speech. The use of metaphors in Arabic and Tashelhiyt reflected this. And, he continued, this also explains the other stuff you've been asking about [i.e., the hermeneutic veil]. We access reality through speech and speech is unreliable. You can't trust it. That's why we can't know what other people think inside.

Language is untrustworthy and, insofar as the people that produce it are unknowable, so are they. It is this radical uncertainty about the nature of communication, and what Goffman called the "transformational vulnerability" of the interactive frames thus established, that gives rise to a general ideology of mistrust. The social implications of this ideology are what we explore in the next chapter.

CHAPTER 2

Trust or tolerance?
On the treachery of friends

La moitié d'un ami, c'est la moitié d'un traître

Half of a friend is always half a traitor

Victor Hugo

One of the central tenets of much of the recent sociological and policy-oriented trust literature is that generalized or socially-extensive trust is correlated with higher levels of tolerance. In its simplest form, this boils down to the perhaps surprising claim that the more likely one is to agree with the statement "most people can be trusted," the more one is inclined to accept that those people are somehow different from oneself—be that in terms of religion, skin color, sexual orientation, or political stripe. The underlying idea is that insofar as people assume that beneath the superficial difference other people are fundamentally similar to themselves, the greater the chance that they will consider them trustworthy.[1] This correlation of trust and tolerance is then frequently extended to embrace the purportedly related values of freedom and equality (Sztompka 1999), as well as social ideals or practices like transparency or liberalism, and

---

1. Although, as so often in the social psychology literature, the question of what precisely people trust others (not) to do is normally left unanswered. Do they trust them not to kidnap their children? Not to steal their bike? To tell the truth?

even psychological states such as self-esteem (Sullivan et al. 1982). Finally, this whole conceptual edifice of values is often presented as girdered by the structuring frame of social capital (Borgonovi 2012), understood in the rather loose and generally positive sense of Putnam (1993) as the sum of all social networks within a given community and the norms of reciprocity they foster.[2] And, as I shall argue, these extensive and ramifying networks of social capital can be seen, from a historical perspective, as a by-product of the emergence of friendship as a fundamental ordering principle of society (cf. Silver 1990). What we have then is an ideal social architecture in which the twin pillars of trust and tolerance that prop up civil society are themselves buttressed by modern forms of liberal democratic sociality. It is the taken-for-granted quality of this three-way relationship that we explore in this chapter.

I suggest that while *social* trust may indeed breed *social* tolerance, it can also on a personal level make people extremely intolerant of lapses or failings in their relationships with intimate others. One of the most striking aspects of trust is its rather absolutist quality: as has often been remarked (e.g., Abraham Lincoln's famous speech at Clinton, Illinois in 1854), you only need to betray or mislead somebody once (or, as with the boy who cried wolf, perhaps twice) to become permanently untrustworthy. Trust not only supposes, but actively demands reliability, and can be extremely unforgiving when it is not forthcoming. The situation is, however, different in a place like the Moroccan High Atlas where, as we have seen, people are not supposed to be trustworthy. To the contrary, others (and even very intimate others) are *expected* to lapse and sometimes fail: to betray their friends, break their word, and let people down. This is not to imply that such betrayals simply go unnoticed. If you prick an Ashelḥiy, he will of course bleed; if you wrong him, however, he is, I think, more likely to be tolerant and perhaps forgiving of the fault—at least in his intimate relations. This form of mistrusting tolerance can, I argue, be seen, in a sense, as radically liberal in its acceptance of the other's right not be predictable (the key generator of trust) or reliable and not to be bound by the actions and assurances of its past self. Mistrust, rather than being the necessary enemy of tolerance and freedom, can also enable them. This comes across particularly clearly in

---

2.   This, of course, is somewhat different to the more technical (and interesting) use of the term by Bourdieu (1980), where social capital refers to the quasi-institutionalized network of relations upon which an individual can draw in his efforts to maximize his chances in the great social game.

practices of friendship[3] and in the management of betrayal, and so it is with these that we begin.

Amity undone

*The journey from the base-town of Demnate to the village of Tiflilist covers little more than a hundred miles, but it takes roughly four hours, as the battered and overloaded Mercedes minibus stutters over high-mountain passes and repeatedly pauses to pick up and drop off its human and sometimes ovine cargo. On this occasion, in May 2012, I decided to alight an hour before we reached our destination and pay a visit to an old friend of mine, a school teacher called Rachik. During the time I had lived in Tiflilist, we had been extremely close. We had spent innumerable mornings sitting on the steps outside the makeshift school-building where he ought to have been teaching, discussing village affairs with one another, with passers-by, and most of all with two other close friends of ours from Tiflilist itself: 'Ali and 'Abd al-Hamid. Together, the four of us had whiled away the winter hours, held dinner-parties (*zzerda*) in my hut, visited other villages, and gone on carpet-buying trips to the parched Moroccan south. And their intimacy had continued and perhaps even strengthened over the years since I had returned to Europe, though it had also settled into that comfortable and, as we shall see, somewhat disabused friendship born of long acquaintance.*

*Rachik was from the fertile Berber-speaking plains to the north-east of Tiflilist and, like many Moroccans, he cultivated the dream of one day returning to his natal village (*tamazirt*). But unless he marries and has children, and for the moment he insists that marriage is the last thing on his mind, it is unlikely he will ever accumulate enough administrative points to be transferred out of the mountains. After eight years in Tiflilist, however, he longed for a change of scenery and applied for a transfer to another nearby school. The move only brought him ten miles closer to plains, but more importantly it took him to a village with electricity (i.e., a television) and greatly improved transport links; and just as importantly it gave him some much*

---

3. Mistrust is, as I have already suggested, also very present in kinship relations. The more intimate of these, however, are also seriously constrained by economic and social factors: if one is betrayed by a coresident brother, one may very well still have to rub along with him. This makes friendship (which often overlaps with some form of kinship) a more obvious place to explore the impact of mistrust and betrayal on people's behavior.

needed distance from what he decried as the scandal-mongering, back-biting and deleterious climate of gossip (tabergagt) *that reigned in Tiflilist.*

For years, he claimed to have been unjustly accused of sowing the seeds of social discord by carrying on with his fellow teachers,[4] *making eyes at girls both eligible and ineligible, and generally prowling about the place like a hungry jackal in search of a lamb. These accusations and his supposed fear of some of the locals had, he claimed, forced him to walk with eyes constantly downturned whenever he left the school compound and he had been unable to move to a more comfortable house in the village for fear of being charged with immoral sexual conduct* (zzīna).

To make matters worse, he suspected our good friend 'Abd al-Hamid, and to a lesser extent 'Ali, of being behind many of these rumors and this undercurrent of tension placed periodic strain on their relationships. Nevertheless, they remained close and even after the move Rachik continued to visit Tiflilist from time to time to spend an evening with them and in particular with 'Ali for whom he reserved special affection. They were closer in age, more worldly and shared a similar blend of social cynicism, intellectual disdain for their peers, Amazigh cultural romanticism, and questing humor that made them well suited to one another.

It was, in any case, in his new village of Yufghid that I was now visiting Rachik. Having left the minibus, I wandered over to the school buildings and peered in through the shattered windows of various classrooms until I located Rachik's. We greeted one another and then he sent the children home early for the day so we could go back to his place (just outside the village proper, but not in the school compound) and catch up. Rachik tends to the taciturn and, as we have seen, people in a local context are anyway very far from forthcoming about their personal lives. So the catching up swiftly petered out. Instead, I asked Rachik if he'd like to come with me to Tiflilist the next day. We could walk the scenic route through the mountains and spend the evening with 'Abd al-Hamid and 'Ali. He paused, and then said, "I can't go to Tiflilist. There's a problem." I raised an eyebrow and enquired as to the problem and, after very little persuasion, Rachik offered me a narrative replete with precisely the kind of rich detail that is typically absent from the kinds of discourse discussed in the previous chapter. It was, in other words, a narrative that mattered and that wanted to be believed.

---

4. I cannot speak to the accuracy of the other rumors, but this one at least was not without foundation. It is also worth noting that, whilst Rachik's complaints were undoubtedly exaggerated, other teachers (who as outsiders are systematically the object of such pernicious gossip) had previously been hounded from the village (see chapter 3).

Rachik had visited Tiflilist two months previously in order to pay his respects and offer his commiserations to 'Ali on the premature death of his coresident "brother" (in fact his patrilateral parallel cousin), taken from this world by a cough. Now for several months prior to this trip, Rachik had been receiving strange text messages from an unknown number, enquiring after his health, wishing him a pleasant 'ayd, *and generally displaying a degree of solicitude that bordered on the intimate. Strangely enough, and contrary to standard Moroccan practice,[5] he had never taken the trouble to find out who his covert friend or secret admirer might be. Or so he claimed. Given the argument outlined in the previous chapter, we would perhaps do best to place this entire account in a state of suspended veracity; at least until we have glimpsed the other side of the story.*

In any case, he decided to walk the three hours to Tiflilist and for most of his journey, he walked alone. As he neared his destination, however, he ran into Rabi'a, the daughter of 'Abd al-Hamid, and they kept one another company for the last half hour or so. As they walked, Rabi'a revealed to him that it was she who had been sending the mysterious text messages. Rachik contested this claim, as the Arabic was very good and Rabi'a (now in her mid-twenties) was too old to have received much formal schooling. Rabi'a replied that she had looked the correct formulae up in books. Rachik then added that "She also told me about how two men from Ayt Mhand had tried to sexually assault the local nurse *[a young French girl based in Tiflilist]" and he looked at me pointedly. Uncomprehending, I replied,* "So what?" *and Rachik explained that the act of recounting the assault to an unrelated man displayed a lack of "shame" (*ḥshuma—*i.e., sexual decorum) that can only have been designed to excite him to lust.[6]*

Upon reaching the village, they went their separate ways: Rabi'a about her business and Rachik to the house of 'Ali where he presented his commiserations and a small gift. The two men spent the rest of the day together, but in the evening, they went over to 'Abd al-Hamid's house, as his extended family has an ornate

---

5. See Carey (2012) for a comprehensive discussion of Moroccan strategies surrounding anonymous phone calls and text messages—basically, one should always follow up on them.

6. This might seem a slightly bizarre interpretation, but it makes sense locally. Several of the teachers informed me that one local seduction technique involved meeting a woman alone in the mountain and running her down; if she allowed herself to be caught, then she accepted the union. I don't necessarily set much store by the truth of this claim, but the fact that the teachers seemed to believe it makes Rachik's reading of the conversation (if, in fact, it occurred) slightly more comprehensible.

collective guest room (tamesrit) *where visitors to the village often stay. The three men ate together and a little after nine, both 'Ali and 'Abd al-Hamid retired for the night, leaving Rachik alone in the guest room and locking the outermost of the two doors to protect him from thieves (see chapter 4). He soon dozed off, only to awake an hour later when he heard a key turning in the lock. He called out to the intruder, asking who it was, but there was no reply ... until a few seconds later when who but Rabi'a should slip into the room, bearing a candle. (Such a situation is, of course, wholly improper in the context of the High Atlas, even bearing in mind the close friendship between Rachik and 'Abd al-Hamid, his long and easy familiarity with Rabi'a, and her uncommonly forthright and independent behavior.) As such, Rachik did his utmost to persuade her that she should leave immediately, that the situation was compromising, and that somebody might walk in on them. But Rabi'a would not listen. She replied that she just wanted to talk a little. And talk she did, for a time ... but inching closer all the while until at last she tried to slip under the blankets with Rachik. He resisted; she insisted; he stood firm; and at last she withdrew, this time locking the innermost of the two doors—the one that leads from the guest room to the antechamber and thence to several different possible exits.*

For the rest of the night, Rachik scarcely slept, but lay there and worried over the potential consequences of Rabi'a's intemperate behavior. When dawn came and the village began to stir, he arose and waited to be released, but nobody came. Nobody brought him tea or breakfast and nobody unlocked the door. Six o'clock came and went, then seven, then eight o'clock. The window of the guest room looked out over the collective courtyard (asarag) of the extended family, but he was too frightened to call openly for help. Finally, towards nine, he spotted 'Abd al-Hamid and Rabi'a whispering suspiciously to one another at the other side of the asarag. *Fear gripped him. At last he saw one of the young boys of the family crossing the courtyard and signaled to him. The boy came closer and Rachik asked to be released. Once out of the guest room, he didn't take the main exit through the courtyard, but slipped silently out the back way, via the lavatory. Heart beating fast, he made his way down through the village unnoticed, but as he neared the river, he heard 'Abd al-Hamid's voice calling out his name. And without turning, he started to run.*

As he ran, his telephone began to ring, but he ignored it. When he had put a good few miles between himself and the supposed ire of 'Abd al-Hamid (who is well over seventy years old), he slowed to walking pace and looked at his phone. It was the same mysterious number that had previously sent him all the text messages. It rang again; he answered and immediately hung up. And again; he did the same, hoping to exhaust the caller's credit. At last his phone stopped ringing, and an hour later, he made it to the safety of his home. Later that day, he tried to phone 'Ali to find out what was going on, but this time it was his turn to have his calls ignored. He tried again several times over the next two weeks, but on each occasion, there was no reply. When at last 'Ali did deign to respond, he feigned bafflement and claimed to have no idea what Rachik was talking about.

"Is that what he said?" *I murmured, neutrally.* "Yes," Rachik continued, "and you know why?" *I demurred.* "I found out from some other villagers that 'Ali had been telling 'Abd al-Hamid and Rabi'a that I wanted to marry her."—"Is that so?"—"Yes! Because he has been screwing her for years. How many times have people walked into the collective granary and caught him lying on top of her (*ign flass*)?" *I nodded and decided to abandon the idea of his accompanying me to Tiflilist the next day.*

This, I think we can safely say, is as clear cut an example as one could hope to find of friendship and of trust betrayed. Rachik's two closest friends in the mountains, whom he had known for ten years, had conspired to catch him up in a shot-gun wedding of sorts, one of them so as to cover up his own sexual misdemeanors and the other so as to fob his no-longer-nubile daughter (a girl to whom, I should point out in the interests of full disclosure, I was extremely close) off on this relatively wealthy and guileless teacher from the plains. At least that is the case if we believe Rachik's side of the story. The other side, which was related to me the next day by 'Abd al-Hamid (partly in the presence of Rabi'a) when I reached Tiflilist, was of an attempted rape conducted under the protection afforded by hospitality and then a cowardly retreat beaten when morning came. Whichever side of the tale is closest to the truth, this is no minor betrayal, but one that confronts some of the core values of local life, such as hospitality and freedom or autonomy. The fallout from this affair also speaks, in a roundabout way, to the question of tolerance and this is something to which we shall return, but first we need to explore in a little more depth the nature of the conceptual relationship between our three key terms of trust, tolerance, and friendship.

THE TIES THAT BIND

This idea of a necessary connection between trust and tolerance is, as mentioned, less self-evident than it is frequently made to appear. On the one hand, the fact that they are so frequently evoked in the same breath, and the seamless way they intersect with the political imaginary of liberal democracy, does make them a compelling pair. Modern democracies, at least in their self-representation, endeavor to cluster around an ideological pole comprising these values and the related notions of freedom, transparency, and equality mentioned above, contrasting themselves *en bloc* with authoritarian political systems which are seen as signally lacking in these cardinal virtues. It seems to stands to reason that trust and tolerance complement one another.

On a more practical level, however, it is far from clear how these different terms are causally related to one another and the ample literature (e.g., Putnam et al. 1993; Seligman 2011) discussing them rarely in fact offers anything more than simple correlation. Why is it that trust should breed tolerance or vice versa? If we think back to the introductory chapter, interpersonal trust is frequently presented as a product of familiarity. In order to trust, we need to believe ourselves more or less capable of predicting another's action and have a feel for the way they would act in a given situation. Perhaps the surest and most straightforward way of doing this is through *identification*: how would I act in this circumstance? The more that others are seen as similar to oneself, the easier it is to imagine their possible courses of action and so to trust them. This being so, we might expect to find greater degrees of extended social trust in more homogeneous societies; there is, however, no particular reason why these more homogeneous societies should be more tolerant than diverse ones. Indeed, the research actually suggests quite the opposite. Whether we examine the macrosociological level of cities and empires (Nederman 2000) or the microsociology of schooling and education (e.g., Janmaat 2010; Rydgren et al. 2013), all the evidence suggests that greater exposure to diversity increases tolerance.

Trust and tolerance, then, would seem to be at conceptual loggerheads, as the former is fostered by social homogeneity and the latter by heterogeneity. So we return to the question of what in fact links the two terms. And the answer is that rather than being seen as directly related, they are often independently associated with a particular social technology: social capital (e.g., Svendsen and Svendsen 2009). The idea in an nutshell is that members of communities or societies with more ramifying networks of social relations—often ones that cut across different forms of social, religious, or ethnic divide—are more likely to display both tolerance and trust towards their peers. In contrast, societies where there are few if any binding ties beyond the immediate nuclear family (cf. Banfield 1958) have been portrayed as incapable of extending trust to nonintimates. This idea that extensive social networks are generative of trust and tolerance and that the three work in harmony to strengthen the bonds of civil society is, it should be noted, quite extraordinarily apolitical, insofar as it ignores the central role played by the state in creating a favorable climate for, and so guaranteeing or underwriting, interpersonal relations. It also (and perhaps unsurprisingly in an age of neoliberal ideology) has an extremely zeitgeisty feel to it, and the recent explosion of interest in these questions is quite unprecedented. It is not, however, a new idea. Indeed, as Allan Silver (1990) so brilliantly demonstrates in his classic work on the question, such associations are in fact one of the cornerstones of liberal modernity and sink their roots right the way back to the Scottish Enlightenment and to authors such as Hume, Ferguson, and Adam Smith.

TRUST AS ARTICULATED SYMPATHY

These authors, particularly Adam Smith, are perhaps most commonly thought of as theorists of the market and, moreover, of a very particular kind of market: one in which intervention is kept to a minimum, except to prevent the formation of cartels, and the system largely regulates itself thanks to the homeostatic effects of unbridled competition. This is the now familiar, and once more sharply apolitical, idea that by creating a space in which every man can act in his own self-interest, regardless of personal ties and sentiment, the greater good is served. In Smith's famous words:

> It is not from the benevolence of the butcher, the brewer, or the baker, that we expect our dinner, but from their regard to their own interest. We address ourselves, not to their humanity but to their self-love, and never talk to them of our own necessities but of their advantages. (1976 [1776]: 26–7)

This, it might reasonably be supposed, is a hard-nosed philosophy of atomized individualism quite alien to the ideas of trust, tolerance, and social capital mentioned above. But it is only half the story of Scottish Enlightenment thought. As Silver reminds us, these thinkers were also quite clear that such ruthless self-interest should be very tightly restricted to the commercial sphere, thereby freeing up space for a purely disinterested form of relationship: friendship. And this friendship was understood as voluntary, egalitarian, personal, and based on an affective bond. In other words, it is a tie contracted between people who consider themselves (for the purposes of the relationship) equals, who relate to one another as individuals (rather than as representatives of particular social or status groups), and who freely choose to associate on the basis of what Smith calls "sympathy."

This notion of sympathy is critical. It is first introduced by Hume in his *Treatise of human nature* (1738) but it is in the work of Adam Smith that it receives the fullest attention: his first book, *The theory of moral sentiments* (*TMS*, 2002 [1759]), is essentially an extended disquisition on the nature and action of sympathy, which he sees as the foundation of human sociality. He defines it most minimally as "fellow-feeling with any passion whatever" (*TMS* I.i.1.5)— i.e., as something akin to what we would now call empathy, or the capacity to feel *with* another.[7] Recognizably related ideas concerning the centrality of empathy to social existence, and the inevitability of "participation" in the inner worlds of others, have recently resurfaced in the anthropological literature (e.g., Hollan and Throop 2008, 2011; Bloch 2015), partly in response to the discovery of "mirror neurons"—i.e., the fact that identical neurons are fired by performing an action (such as crying or pointing) and observing somebody else perform it. This, in the words of Hollan and Throop, suggests a "previously unimagined and remarkable capacity to *participate*, indirectly and passively, in the movements and actions of others" (2011: 1, emphasis added). Smith, however, was not primarily interested in the alchemical transmission of passion from one person to another, as he insisted that passions (or emotional states) in fact communicate themselves rather imperfectly between people. We may, he observed, quite fail to share another's joy or, conversely, experience a passion on his behalf of which he appears incapable (*TMS* I.i.1.9–10).

Instead, Smith focuses his attention on the role of imaginative projection in the communion of human passion, whereby a witness to another's sorrow or joy "changes places in fancy" (*TMS* I.i.1.3) with the person experiencing the passion. We imagine ourselves in the other's situation and experience what we imagine we would feel—in short, we *identify* with the position they find themselves in and ideally with their response to it.[8] This corresponds rather more

---

7.   See, for instance, Griswold (1999) or Weinstein (2013) for a much fuller discussion of the concept.

8.   This actually raises a very nice question about the object of such identification. Smith, for instance, discusses the limit-case of sympathy with the dead, where we "are chiefly affected by those circumstances which strike our senses, but can have no influence upon their happiness. It is miserable, we think, to be deprived of the light

closely with the latter half of Halpern's definition of empathy as "a type of reasoning in which a person emotionally resonates with the experience of another while simultaneously attempting to imaginatively view a situation from that other person's perspective" (paraphrased in Hollan and Throop 2011: 2). Here the focus is less on participation in the other's inner world and more on the complex and extended process of *identification* that is the work of empathy. It is, in any case, this idea of identification or imaginative projection that interests Smith and that underpins his concept of sympathy and so friendship.

In schematic terms, then, friendship is predicated upon sympathy and sympathy is predicated upon identification with the other's response to a given situation. And understood in this sense, we can also argue that this process of identification can be seen as the present tense equivalent of the anticipation of and identification with the other's future responses to a situation which is the base mechanism of trust. Sympathy requires the capacity to "change places in fancy" and so identify with the other in the here and now, whilst trust relies on the ability to project this process of identification into the future and so foresee the other's disposition or even future action.[9] *Sympathy is trust in the present and trust is sympathy extended into the future.*

It is, then, no coincidence, that these Scottish Enlightenment thinkers also place trust and intimacy (the progressive unveiling of oneself to another) right at the heart of friendship. Indeed, Adam Ferguson goes so far as to describe friendship as characterized by "unlimited confidence" and suggests that any loss of faith in this confidence must cause the friendship to end (cited in Silver 1990: 1486). And it is this again somewhat absolute form of friendship, constructed as we have seen on the solid ground of individuality, equality, choice, sympathy, disinterestedness, and trust, that serves as the social technology binding

---

of the sun; to be shut out from life and conversation; to be laid in the cold grave, a prey to corruption and the reptiles of the earth" (*TMS* I.i.1.13). In this case, it might seem that the person himself is almost entirely irrelevant to the action of sympathy and the only thing that matters is the situation, but Smith immediately quashes this line of reflection by turning his attention to the higher pleasure of mutual sympathy, thus placing the person qua person back at the center of things.

9. Just as mistrust can, as mentioned above, take two forms (the assumption that the other is unknowable or that he is knowable but his intentions are malign), so trust can rely on the idea that the other's actions are foreseeable or that they are unforeseeable, but his disposition is good—one can rely on him to do the right thing). The sympathetic quality of trust covers both of these possibilities.

together the whole of civil society (another central category in Scottish En-lightenment thought).[10]

Just as the Balinese *Negara*, glossed by Geertz as the "Theatre-State" (1980), acted as an exemplary center unifying and exerting a centripetal force upon the entire Balinese polity, so friendship is here the exemplary center of social rela-tions, which acts to unify all others. Those same qualities that are definitional of friendship are extended, in attenuated form, to the gamut of social interac-tions: from bosom friends to casual acquaintances and thence to strangers. For the modern commercial society described by these Enlightenment thinkers is fundamentally one composed of strangers, but unlike other early theorists of modernity (both conservative and radical), they see this not as a recipe for ano-mie and disintegration, but an opportunity for a more *civil* society. In the words of Silver, "[f]or Smith, sympathy makes possible the creation and coordina-tion of moral action in an individuated society no longer morally governed by prince, clergy, and landlord [...] It is a procedural mechanism, without intrinsic emotional or moral content. People moderate their behavior to attract others' sympathy" (1990: 1482). In short, they act towards one another as potential friends, treating others as equal individuals to whom one is initially indifferent, but for whom one may be moved to disinterested sympathy and to whom one might conceivably extend trust.

The clear contrast here is with the world of pre-commercial society, both in its small-scale traditional incarnations and in the more elaborate form of the *ancien régime*. In contexts where commercial activities are not tightly seg-regated from wider flows of social existence,[11] Smith argues, friendship cannot be truly voluntary and disinterested.[12] Instead, it always overlaps with interested forms of behavior; it is always partly born of convenience or necessity. Nor is it restricted to particular categories of people defined by their position, role, or

---

10. It is perhaps worth noting, in passing, that the idea that friendship might serve as a basis for all social ties in fact has a pedigree stretching as far back as Aristotle's *The ethics*; for Aristotle, however, the highest form of friendship is predicated on unselfish virtue, where one merely wants what's best for one's fellow man, rather than on the Enlightenment idea of sympathy.

11. It is not my purpose here to enter into debate about the relationship between economic activity and social life, but I should note that this is, in the wake of Polanyi (1944), a vast field of inquiry.

12. Just think of classical anthropological ideas of the gift, where person and exchange are entirely inextricable (cf. Mauss 1968 [1923–24]).

status, but as it depends on the action of sympathy, it can potentially embrace all and sundry. Only in a society composed of liberal, equal individuals can friendship fully flourish and only in such a society can it serve as a template for social relations in their entirety.

An anthropological intermezzo

It is worth noting, in passing, that this notion of friendship has been the object of a good deal of criticism, notably from within anthropology. Much of this criticism has predictably involved efforts to destabilize this rather totalizing vision of friendship, by pointing out, first, that friendship can and does exist in non-commercial societies and, second, that it can exist in the absence of many of these supposedly key attributes. So Killick (2010) argues, based on his Amazonian fieldwork, that friendship is not necessarily contracted between equals, but can also stretch to encompass asymmetrical relationships between, say, indigenous loggers and mestizo traders. Friendship, in these instances, is attached to other institutional relations like compradazgo *(godparenthood) and acquires something of their form; Lebner (2012) makes a similar point when she suggests that the archetype of friendship on the Brazilian frontier is not with a peer, but with God. Others have argued that friendship may not always be chosen on the basis of sympathy, but more or less determined by objective sociological factors like coevality, as with same-year siblingship in southern China (Santos 2008) or propinquity, as in Froerer's (2010) study of rural Indian friendships between women. And many more have pointed out that institutions of bond friendship found in parts of Africa (e.g., Shack 1963) and elsewhere (e.g., Firth 1967) make friendships partially or completely indissoluble; by linking them to other institutions, they become less flexible and harder to break at will. These points are, in the main, valid and interesting, but they can also be seen as ultimately serving to strengthen the Scottish Enlightenment argument that it is only in modern liberal societies (or those that resemble them on a number of levels) that friendship in the sense outlined above can flourish.*

It is, in any event, this constellation of ideas that, as we have seen, informs much of the modern trust literature with its claims of a confluence of trust and tolerance, although the strong Enlightenment emphasis on the social technology of friendship is typically muted in favor of a focus on social capital and civil society (which we can think of as friendship in its extended or attenuated form). Liberal societies where social capital is high and trust is extensive tend, so the argument goes, to be more tolerant because the ramifying networks of social capital are composed of individuals who extend trust to one another qua individuals and not, ideally, to individuals qua representatives of a particular social type (Whites, heterosexuals, Lutherans, etc.). The difference of "state" is accepted (or "tolerated") because people extend trust to other people *who share the same quality as individuals*.

This, of course, is a highly idealized picture, which corresponds only very imperfectly to the reality of social relations on the ground, but it is, crucially, an idealized vision that is often shared by both researchers and the people they study. Most people in those liberal societies that display the highest levels of extended social trust and tolerance (countries such as Sweden or the Netherlands)[13] would doubtless like to think that they chose their friends based on sympathy, rather than religion or race, and this is reflected in their increased discursive tolerance. The Scottish Enlightenment model of friendship and society is both model of and model for liberal modernity, both feeding off and fostering the association of trust and tolerance. But whilst this association may well hold good at the broader social level, I would argue that the omnipresence of an ideology of trust also works against tolerance when it comes to personal relations.

For the ideology of trust that underpins modern and liberal forms of friendship has not only stretched out to colonize the realm of wider social relations; it has also been turned inward and been used to restructure the domain of intimate relations. Ties such as those of kinship, marriage, and alliance that were formerly conceived of in terms of rights, duties, and obligations have been radically reconfigured along novel lines and are now largely conceptualized as based on the ideas of trust, mutual sympathy and voluntary association previously seen as proper to friendship. Indeed, Giddens (1992) sees the intimacy between partners as the acme of those modern values of trust and autonomy. It is no longer surprising to hear Northern Europeans from all walks of life describing their partner or their mother as "my best friend" (cf. Brain 1976).[14] Trust, then,

---

13. At least according to the European Values Study 2008 (http://www.
    europeanvaluesstudy.eu/page/survey-2008.html).

14. It is worth underlining the cultural specificity of such ideas. When I presented a
    preliminary version of this chapter in southern France, a colleague leapt to his feet

has been placed at the heart of these relations, simultaneously breathing new life into them and rendering them hugely more fragile. Relationships built on trust are flimsy and potentially fleeting things when compared to those built on rights and duties, because trust is so unforgiving, so intolerant of betrayal. And betrayal is a fact of human life.

And with that, we can leave Northern Europe and return at last to the Moroccan High Atlas and return to the tale of friendship and betrayal with which we began this chapter. In order, however, to understand how it relates to the foregoing discussion, we need to ask what friendship amounts to in the local context: what does it look like and what role does it play?

UNFATHOMABLE FRIENDS

The High Atlas of the early 2000s was as uncontroversial an example as one could hope to find of a pre-commercial society in the sense of Adam Smith—i.e., one in which there is no clear separation between the conceptual space of the market and the space of sociability and so no clear distinction between interested and disinterested relations, between business partners and friends.[15] To the contrary, relations are there to be instrumentalized and there is no shame in this. I recall wandering through the backstreets of Marrakech with a friend one torrid afternoon and knocking on countless doors in an effort to find the house of a mountain guide he had vaguely known some thirty years earlier. My friend was not especially forthcoming when I inquired as to the purpose of his visit, and I assumed it was the tyrant nostalgia come knocking at his aging frame. But when we finally found the house of this distant acquaintance and were let into the cool interior, practically the entire audience, after the first five minutes of obligatory greetings, was devoted to the question of whether he could find a job for my friend's feckless wastrel of a son. I suspect I was alone in finding this a little awkward. And I, too, was endlessly implored by various friends to find jobs either for them or their

---

when I made this point and insisted that it couldn't possibly be true that parents and children refer to one another as their best friends. Upon my assuring him that it was, he reluctantly sat back down muttering "But that's a category error!"

15. I am not, of course, suggesting that it in any way lies outside the commercial circuits proper to modern capitalism. Much local income comes from cash crops, migrant labor, and NGOs. I am simply stating that the way in which these commercial relations are locally managed looks a lot like Smith's idea of precommercial society.

young relatives; my insistence that I could not simply ask a local farmer back "home" in rural England to take one of them on as a swineherd was considered to be a barefaced lie. I had relations and must, therefore, be able to make something of them, just as they were trying to make something of their friendship with me. To borrow the language of Strathern, the whole point of flows of amical affection is that they can potentially be transformed into flows of money and vice versa.[16] Indeed, this instrumental bent is such a widespread characteristic of Moroccan sociality that it has driven anthropologists such as Rabinow (1977: 48–50) to decry Moroccan friendship as purely instrumental (see below).

The High Atlas is also a space where many aspects of existence are dominated by kinship. The local economy revolves principally around agriculture, arboriculture, and stockherding and these are forms of property that are either owned, managed, and worked at the level of the extended family or, in nucleated households, inherited. Land is only sold when there are no male offspring and livestock are seen principally as reservoirs of wealth rather than tradable goods.[17] Tourism is an important source of revenue in certain parts of the High Atlas, but not where I worked, and all other major sources of income involve leaving the area. As such, the fabric of local economic life is largely structured by kinship and this has considerable knock-on effects on whom one spends one's time with. If you and your second cousin own contiguous fields in a distant valley, it makes sense to plow them together; if you each own half of a walnut tree, you might as well harvest and process the nuts at the same time. What is more, marriage is also very often a corporate affair and frequently contracted within extended families, although love matches are sometimes allowed, particularly in poorer households where the financial implications of marriage are less serious. And finally, many of the smaller villages are made up of only one extended family and intervillage rivalry is nowadays rather fierce.[18] All of this means that

---

16. See Moya (2015) for a more explicitly Melanesianist and instrumentalist discussion of this phenomenon in the Senegalese context, where he argues that the mobilization of flows of money is essential to the generation and maintenance of friendships.

17. This, of course, is a standard trope of pastoral societies. See chapter 5, "The Bovine Mystique," of Ferguson's *The anti-politics machine* (1994) for a comparable situation in Lesotho, where livestock and cash are not freely interconvertible and the close relationship between male prestige and livestock holdings makes it difficult to liquidate them.

18. It used formerly to operate principally between tribal sub-fractions (comprising several villages), but the increase in the size of villages over recent decades,

a goodly part of one's social network and interactions is, if not determined, at least restricted by kinship.[19]

In this sort of situation, friendship clearly cannot play the same structuring role as in a liberal democracy. What is more, kinship and friendship have often been presented as more or less antithetical terms, both from a historical (Adams and Allan 1998; Oliker 1998) and an ethnographic (e.g. Gulliver 1971) perspective, with the former giving ground where the latter waxes strong. Nevertheless, as authors such as Rodgers (2010) and Obeid (2010) have shown, friendship may also be highly valued in contexts where the ties of kinship structure daily life and can sometimes be experienced as personally oppressive.[20] In other words, where people live with, work with, and marry their kin, where kinship is the inescapable cornerstone of much of their existence, then they may look to their friends to provide them with light-hearted and affectionate company. Now, I do not think that ideas of friendship (*tiddukla*) in the High Atlas are so strictly opposed to kinship in general (and there is frequently considerable overlap between the two categories), but friendship is certainly an extremely salient local category, both conceptually and practically. There are a number of reasons for this.

First, friends are people with whom one can be at ease, whereas relations between especially close male kin are marked (as in many other parts of the wider Middle East) by questions of shame. In the presence of close agnatic kin or relatives by alliance of a different generation, people with whom they are in close and unequal relations, men are supposed rigidly to police their behavior, adopting particular postures, avoiding any ribald or controversial topics of conversation, and generally maintaining a respectful silence. Any breaching of these conventions may be emotionally intolerable. For instance, the night before I left the

---

coupled with vastly improved links to the plains, has shifted the level of primary identification down to the village or hamlet (cf. Carey 2007).

19. Of course, as the longstanding body of work on "relatedness" (Carsten 2000) has convincingly shown, kinship permits of a good degree of flexibility and choice, but structures of residence and inheritance in the High Atlas only permit of so much variation.

20. A very similar point was made as far back as 1969 by Robert Paine, when he criticized the standard opposition between friendship societies and kinship societies, noting that it may be precisely in contexts "where kinship roles are ambiguous and optative … [that] affective exchange takes place in the voluntary and revocable relations of friendship" (508).

village in 2005, after having lived there for sixteen months, I invited a few close friends over to my house for a valedictory dinner and unthinkingly included an uncle and nephew in the small party. The uncle chose to spend the entire evening sat in the corridor in subzero temperatures, warming his hands at a little brasero, in case somebody cracked a blue joke. Relations between female kin are somewhat more relaxed, and are not in any case marked by such obvious patterns of avoidance, but they are still hierarchical across generations and complicated by questions of obligation and duty, which trouble the ideally seamless flow of sociality. Friends, in contrast, enjoy easy, egalitarian relations that allow conversation to flit dizzily and pleasingly from topic to topic. It is in such conversation that the pleasant company discussed in the previous chapter consists: the expressions *iḥla wawal* (the words are good) and *ifulki wawal* (the words are beautiful) are used both to reflect contentedly on time well spent and to reassure somebody worried that the verbal jousting might have gone too far that things are in fact okay.

Friendship is also important precisely because it can be instrumentalized and because it is more easily extensible than kinship. I have argued elsewhere (Carey 2012) that rural, and probably urban, Moroccan sociality is characterized by the ceaseless attempt to multiply potential networks. This is a world in which there are two paths to success: the impersonal bureaucracy of the postcolonial state and personal connections. The second path is not only more effective and flexible, it is also open to the unschooled masses; the first person from my tribal subfraction to pass the baccalaureate graduated in 2012. As such, it is important to cultivate friends as widely as possible, for as we saw when we went knocking on the doors of Marrakesh, one never knows when they might come in handy. This also perhaps explains the rather broad compass of the word *amdakkal* (friend), which people use to describe everybody from lifelong friends to people they once met at the market. By using a neutral and highly flexible term, one leaves room for renegotiation of the relationship if an opportunity presents itself.

Finally, and perhaps most importantly, friends are companions. Just as among some warlike peoples in Amazonia, such as the Yanomami (Alès 2000) or the Parakanã (Fausto 2012), the archetype of the friend is the *compagnon de guerre*, in the High Atlas it is undoubtedly the traveling companion (*asmun*; *ghwa dak imun*).[21] Whilst people use the word friend (*amdakkal*) rather loosely

---

21. See also Marsden (2009) for a comparative discussion of the centrality of travel to friendship and intimacy in Chitral, northern Pakistan, where young men engage in forms of local travel to appreciate the beauty of their region as well as to escape the

when referring to their own relations, in my experience, the principal situation in which they systematically append it to other people's relations—as in "I was talking to your friend Hamd" (*arr sawalgh d Ḥamd, amdakkalnk*)—is when they have been on a journey together; staying the night at somebody's house is another. It is on journeys, especially long journeys, that one develops familiarity with another's habits, shares vivid experiences, and cultivates intensive forms of intimacy. Traveling involves almost permanent proximity, as people eat, wash, and sleep together, often for very long periods of time. Lifelong friendships are born of such experiences. This is not to suggest that travel is the only way to produce such affectionate familiarity, and static forms of sociability are also characterized by striking physical intimacy (playing with another's feet, falling asleep on people's shoulders) and very extended periods of time amounting to many hours each day spent in each other's company, but travel is the acme of such behavior.

Young men who choose to pursue a religious education still travel together to seminaries (*madāris*) in the south, where they spend long months sharing a room or cell and, in former times, these young men would move from seminary to seminary, sometimes staying away from home for years at a time. Labor migration to the surrounding plains also forges similar bonds. Some young men see it as an opportunity to break with the parochial patterns of mountain life and become proper urbanites, but many travel in pairs and the dyad, rather than the group, is the fundamental unit of friendship. Explaining this to me, one acquaintance jovially pointed at his friend and uttered the immortal line: "*we work together, eat together, sleep together*, nga zund iglay g tlkhisht—*we are like testicles in a sack*." Homoerotic activity is entirely taboo in the area, so whatever the two men may have got up to in their sack, his reference was not to that. Instead, his vivid imagery was an effort to capture the quality of intimacy and affection that such promiscuity generates.

In sum, this idea of friendship shares a number of key attributes with its Scottish Enlightenment equivalent: it may be instrumental, but it is also egalitarian, personalized, and voluntary; it serves as a model for wider social relations in a way that kinship does not, and is based on mutual sympathy and intimacy.[22]

---

narrow confines of mountain life. In so doing, they come to know both their region and one another.

22. This is perhaps not so surprising. Course (2010) argues that Mapuche friendship is also remarkably similar to the liberal Western model, precisely because the Mapuche share an idea of autonomous individualism as the cornerstone of social life. A related point could be made regarding the High Atlas, where this focus on

Crucially, however, this is not an intimacy understood as the "confident revelation of one's inner self to a trusted other" (Silver 1990: 1477). Indeed, how could it be when, as we saw in chapter 1, the idea that the inner self can be fathomed, and by extension exposed, is simply anathema? And without this familiarity with the other's inner world, there can be no pretension to predicting his future behavior and thus no trust in the committal sense outlined above.

This somewhat startling notion that trust might not necessarily be central to ideas and practices of friendship should not be exaggerated. People do, of course, come to know their friends and they do have a feel for how they will behave in various circumstances, even though they might discursively deny it. And if there were no trust whatsoever, then there would, of course, be no sense of betrayal. Yet there is a word for betrayal (*ghder*) and it is the one that Rachik used when discussing 'Ali's behavior. He considered himself to have been betrayed and betrayed badly: he insisted to me that his life had been in danger and that it was no longer safe for him to return to Tiflilist. He had, as the peerless Tashelhiyt idiom has it, been "forced to squat on a sugar loaf" (*isgurm-as f lqalb n sukkar*), betraying his trust on a very basic level. So trust is not, of course, entirely absent from friendship; it is rather that it is neither essential to the relationship, nor definitional of it.

The truly startling thing about the whole episode was not the betrayal itself, but its aftermath. For when I returned to the area a year later, Rachik and 'Ali were once again the very best of friends. Rachik and I walked the route I had planned to take the year before, stopping at 'Ali's high-mountain "orchard" where we found 'Ali irrigating his trees. We spent a couple of hours lying in the shade eating unripe peaches and then walked on to 'Ali's house. We dined together and Rachik stayed the night. The reconciliation was complete. But this was not because Rachik had subsequently discovered that 'Ali had not in fact betrayed him; he remained quite convinced of his skullduggery. Nor was it because it was not, in fact, such a radical act of betrayal; the whole episode, as well as having supposedly imperiled Rachik's life was also, as mentioned, a fundamental breach of the major tenets of local existence. Nor, finally, was it because Rachik had forgiven 'Ali: when I asked whether things were settled, he simply

---

autonomous social actors is, as we have seen, buttressed by the notion that other people are fundamentally inscrutable. And see also Carrier (1999), who suggests, in like vein, that there is a strong correlation between ideas of self and styles of friendship.

said that they had been put behind them. No. The reconciliation was possible because the friendship was not predicated on trust. Rachik considered that 'Ali had been trying to cover his own back and that he was the unfortunate collateral damage in a complex social gambit involving 'Abd al-Hamid and his daughter, Rabi'a. People, he recognized, do regrettable things, but this does not mean that one necessarily ceases to be friends with them.

In other words, the mutual sympathy that underpinned their relationship was not one that depended on the ability to imagine oneself in the other's shoes and identify with his responses and choices. Had this been the case, then the radical act of betrayal would have led, as is so often the case in the trusting societies of Northern Europe, to a shock of misrecognition whereby Rachik realized that he had taken his friend for somebody else. But Rachik had not "taken him" for anyone. 'Ali had behaved in an unpredictable way, but that was his right as an autonomous social actor and though it may have imperiled Rachik's life, it had not imperiled their mutual sympathy, which relied not on mutual identification, but in the pleasure of the other's company—which is pleasant precisely because it is *other*. This, as I suggested at the beginning, is a fairly disabused idea of friendship, but it is also an extremely tolerant and a radically liberal one. As Bell and Coleman note, the loyalty and trust that northern Europeans associate with friendship reduce people's options and bind them to particular courses of action and they do so because such ideas of friendship are predicated on there being "no moral separation between friends" (1999: 44). High Atlas practices of friendship, in contrast, recognize the fundamental unpredictability of others. This unpredictability is, of course, precisely that characteristic of Moroccan sociality that is sometimes interpreted as a typically North African "shiftiness"— an "inability" to keep one's word or a base duplicity—and which can complicate relations with Euro-Americans (cf. *infra*). What I am suggesting is that it is better understood as an expression of people's autonomy, freedom, and their right not to be bound by our misconceptions and expectations.

CONCLUSION

The problem of friendship in Morocco or, more precisely, some American anthropologists' problem *with* friendship in Morocco has become something of a staple of the ultra-Atlantic ethnography. The contours of relationships between anthropologist and informant, interlocutor or friend have, of course, always been of interest to a discipline that relies on human relations for data; think of the classic chapter "Muchona the Hornet" in Victor Turner's *In the forest of symbols* (1967), or Casagrande's collective volume, *In the company of man* (1960). But for the generation of symbolic anthropologists that cut its teeth in 1970s Morocco, and whose experimental ethnography heralded the reflexive turn, these relations transformed at times into the central object of ethnography. This tendency reaches its paroxysm in Rabinow's *Reflections on fieldwork in Morocco* (1977), with its excruciating account of the ingenuous ups and downs of the author's burgeoning friendship with a man who had all the attributes of a local pimp, but the close attention to how relationships are conducted reaches much wider (Eickelman 1976; Crapanzano 1980; Dwyer 1982).

These experiences have, in some cases, been spun out into broader reflections on Moroccan friendship itself and the general consensus is that it is, in the words of Rabinow, above all a matter of "brinkmanship" (1977: 49), of intrigue, scheming, and the constant struggle for domination (Crapanzano 1980: 78).[23] As Spadolo delicately puts it in a recent review of the field, these authors tended to dwell "on the agonies rather than the affections" (2011: 739) of their own relationships, detailing how their informants-cum-friends pushed, tested, and probed them to extract the maximum possible benefit (2011: 742–3) and occasionally regretting that they allowed themselves to respond overly harshly in the face of these instrumentalizing pressures (Rabinow 1977: 45). The agonistic interpretation is also favored by Rachik in his vast overview of a hundred years of Moroccan anthropology, although he adopts the contrary stance of condemning the Americans for being "too nice by far" (2012: 242) and contrasting this with his own principled refusal to develop any form of friendship or intimacy whatsoever whilst in the field. Even Spadolo implicitly accepts this general framework, although he seeks to turn attention away from the brinkmanship and to focus instead on the acts of forgiveness that allow people to redeem one another when they have pushed things too far and lines have been crossed; "mistakes ... are quintessential gifts ... [a]nd they are recuperated through ... the act of forgiving" (2011: 754). This forgiveness, he contends, is fundamentally constitutive of friendship both in Morocco and, perhaps, elsewhere (Spadolo 2011).

---

23. This same idea is, in fact, later taken up by Hammoudi (1997) and extended to all Moroccan relations between men, which are, he claims, predicated on the cultural "*diagramme*" of the master–disciple dyad. One party must ultimately dominate and the other submit, although the possibility of an inversion of roles lurks constantly under the surface and occasionally erupts in the form of violence.

My argument is somewhat different. Whilst agreeing with Spadolo's assessment of friendships in Morocco as extremely forgiving, I do not think that this forgiveness is in and of itself constitutive of the friendship; it is better seen as a side-effect of a deep-seated mistrust. Indeed, my experience of friendship in the High Atlas, both my own and those I have observed, is that active forgiveness is not an especially salient category of local amity. God may, at his discretion, forgive people once they are dead, but human forgiveness is very rarely invoked. The only situation in which the term is regularly used is in the formulaic begging of forgiveness that marks the end of a period of hospitality, when the host entreats the guest to pardon his inadequacies (*samhat-agh! samhat-agh!*). It is not, in my experience, uttered in the aftermath of disputes, and settlement is never discussed in these terms. Indeed, as I argued above, Rachik did not actively *forgive* 'Ali. He was, instead, *forgiving* in both senses of the word: tolerant of betrayal and flexible enough to adapt to it. This flexibility and adaptability are the subject of the next chapter.

CHAPTER 3

The triumph of contingency
Anarchism as Realpolitik

Let me begin, in the manner of a political scientist, with a brace of assertions: political systems, insofar as they are concerned with the coordination of people and things, necessarily sediment and reproduce particular configurations or dispositions of trust and mistrust, which in turn foster or stymie different patterns of cooperation. Further, most real-world (as opposed to utopian) systems more or less explicitly proclaim their suspicion of certain aspects of human nature or behavior and rely on, or trust in, the structuring capacity and concentrated coercive potential of particular institutions. Aristocracies and technocracies, for example, tend to mistrust people in their mass incarnations (the crowd, the mob, the demos) and instead plight their troth to particular classes of people possessed of certain distinguishing qualities (the right blood, say, or expertise), as well as to the institutions that reproduce them: private schools, noble families, or elite universities. Liberal democracies, meanwhile, often claim to be wary of individuals—supposing with some justification that power is liable to corrupt them—but trust in the judgment of the people as a whole, backed up by robust and implacable institutions, to keep the corruption in check.[1] In

---

1. This Lockean and Panglossian vision of liberal democracy is, of course, not without its critics; Marxist scholars, such as Miliband (1969), would argue that it only pays lip service to the people, while actually disenfranchising them in favor of a gilded elite.

short, the complex coordination characteristic of human society is almost everywhere presented as dependent upon a combination of trust and the potential
for coercion.[2]

The one apparent exception to this otherwise banal truism is anarchism, for
whilst it shares with democracy a foundational suspicion of the individual, it
differs radically regarding how best to control his *libido dominandi*. Where democracy relies on the comforting apparatus of coercive institutions, anarchism
advocates their entire suppression. The assumption here, one that is rarely made
explicit, is that once the potential for institutional coercion is removed from
the equation, then cooperation can be achieved through trust alone. As Dunn
vigorously puts it: "at its most optimistic anarchism simply consists in the uni-
versalization of trust towards all humans who are not themselves bearers of
concentrated coercive power" (1988: 76). In this sense, anarchism, whose origins
are often traced to the Enlightenment thought of Rousseau, can equally be seen
as a child of the Scottish Enlightenment, in that its utopian endpoint is in es-
sence a maximal extension of the idea of civil society discussed in the previous
chapter—one in which the trust accorded other equal individuals is sufficient
in and of itself to ensure cooperation. The thing that remains unclear in this
picture, however, is just how—by virtue of which mechanism—the foundational
mistrust of the individual (qua potential tyrant) is transformed into this generalized trust of others.

There are obvious parallels here with that other great current of nineteenth-
century utopian thought, Communism, whose founders memorably claimed
that once "a free and equal association of the producers" (Engels 2004 [1884]:
160) had been established, the socialist state would simply wither away leaving
society to manage itself. For Communists, the mechanism that would allow for
this untrammeled and unassisted cooperation was the root-and-branch remold-
ing of the treacherous capitalist individual into a New Communist Man, but
the unrealized nature of the Communist project means that the efficacy of this
proposed solution must remain moot. Anarchism is different: it is not only an
unfulfilled nineteenth-century political project, but also a recurrent object of
ethnographic description "out there," and one that has witnessed a resurgence

---

2.   Autocracies are sometimes discussed as examples of systems from which trust is
      almost absent (e.g., Arendt 1951), but they can also be understood as systems where
      trust is ideally hyper-concentrated in the person of the autocrat or even, as with
      monarchy by divine right, in the deity who legitimates kingly rule.

of interest in recent years (Graeber 2004; Scott 2009; Macdonald 2011). Key to many of these descriptions is the idea that anarchist polities are not mere accidents of history, but willed projects articulated around the *deliberate* design of neutered or non-coercive institutions, of which the classic example is the "powerless Amazonian chief" (Clastres 1974). It is these institutions, which are the organizational expression of what Graeber calls a "counterpower" (2004: 35), as well as people's ideological commitment to them, that can be understood as enabling the critical transition from mistrust to trust.

In this chapter, I take issue with this well-oiled theoretical machine, suggesting that real-world anarchism is less a deliberate political strategy than an emergent product of the kind of pervasive mistrust present in the Moroccan High Atlas. It is, I argue, the erosive effects of this mistrust that adventitiously produce the powerless institutions characteristic of anarchy. In the High Atlas context, this powerlessness consists in the ephemerality of institutions: their inability to project themselves over time and thereby acquire a coercive presence. Finally, I suggest that this ephemerality means they are only oriented to the *ad hoc* and have no embedded ideological tendencies. Anarchy, far from being an ideological project, is in fact closer to a form of contingent Realpolitik. But first, let us consider the political landscape of the region.

THE HIGH ATLAS POLITY

There are two basic interpretations of traditional Atlassian political practice: the anarchic Anglo-Saxon one and the institution-heavy Franco-Moroccan one.[3] For a generation of scholars influenced by Ernest Gellner's seminal *Saints of the Atlas* (1969), it was clear that politics in the region was essentially an artifact of the segmentary lineage system. This meant that there were no clearly differentiated political institutions, but that ties of kinship served instead to manage any problems that arose. The basic idea is that everybody in a given community is related through the male line and that whom one sides with in a conflict is always dictated by how much paternal blood one shares with the protagonists. So, if I quarrel with my paternal cousin, then my immediate family will take my part and his will do the same; but if I quarrel with a more distant relative, then

---

3. See Roberts (2002), for a more detailed presentation of this fundamental opposition from the point of view of neighboring Kabylia.

my cousin and his family will fall in alongside me; and so forth. This idea is reflected in the oft-quoted Arabic saying, "Me against my brother; my brother and me against my cousin; my cousin, my brother, and me against the world." The system is supposed to work because of the ideal nested symmetry of agnatic kinship, which ignores all relations through the female line; this symmetry means that whenever there is a conflict, there should be a relative balance of forces on either side of the equation, preventing any one party from imposing its will. Accordingly, social pressure normally forces a resolution and, if there can be no resolution, then the group simply *segments* and each side goes its separate way. The system is excessively elegant, as fractals typically are.

There are, though, a number of important caveats. First is that the system can only work optimally in nomadic or semi-nomadic societies where there is little or no cost to segmenting; when immovable property and enforced propinquity come into play, splitting a community becomes much more complicated. Second, it notably fails to explain how to manage both intra-familial (when it's me against my brother) and inter-group conflict. Gellner dealt with the latter by appealing to saintly families established on the frontiers between groups, who made use of their religious charisma (*baraka*) to handle such relations and, incidentally, to extract a handsome tribute; but he has precious little to say about the former. What is more, and this is perhaps a legacy of the British colonial system and its impact on Anglo-Saxon anthropology,[4] the theory is *only* concerned with how to manage conflict and maintain control. There is no mention whatsoever of how people might have organized cooperation—when they needed to build a bridge, clear the snow from a mountain pass, or pay for and recruit a religious specialist for their community. All that seems to matter is how to keep the peace beloved of colonial authorities. And for this, kinship alone sufficed. The system was thus clearly anarchic in the straightforward sense that there was no overarching political authority (i.e., it was acephalous) and no alienation of coercion to specialized institutions. It was also immensely popular as an explanation of local politics throughout the 1970s and 1980s; the classic works are by Hart (1976, 1981). Unfortunately, its palpable and repeated failure to conform to the reality of High Atlas life—to give but one crushing example,

---

4.   The most famous example of a segmentary lineage system is, of course, Evans-Pritchard's classic description of the Nuer (1940)—a study undertaken at the behest of the colonial government, who were having trouble quelling the rebellious Nuer and needed a clearer idea of their political system.

most Atlas communities do not claim to be descended from a common ances-
tor and so cannot regulate quarrels by reckoning agnatic kinship—meant that
by the late 1990s, even Hart had been forced to renounce the faith and only
Wolfgang Kraus (1998) kept the lonely flame burning. The High Atlas polity
might have been anarchic, but it was certainly not so in the sense understood
by Ernest Gellner.

In the meantime, attention had turned away from the Anglo-Saxon model
and toward a much older (and notably less anarchic) idea, first proposed by the
French colonial officials Hanoteau and Letourneux (1872–73) for Kabylia, a
Berber-speaking region in neighboring Algeria. They and their numerous fol-
lowers, from Masqueray (1886) to Mahé (2002), argued that Kabyle political
practice was organized around the *ljmā'* (council; Tach. *ajmu'*),[5] an institution
sometimes likened to the Athenian *ecclesia*. The precise composition and functioning of these councils seems to vary, but in broad brushstrokes, it comprised
(and in many cases still comprises) all adult men of a village, who assembled in
a set location on a Friday after midday prayer to decide on village affairs. Attendance was compulsory, procedures tightly regimented, there was an elected
president (*amin*), and the council was mandated to fine those who stepped out
of line. In the early colonial period, these councils also elected representatives
to "super-councils" at the level of the tribal fraction, tribe, and even confedera-
tion (*saff*). These were, in short, fully-fledged and coercive political institutions.
This model, which seems to account quite well for Kabyle political practice,
was subsequently imported from Algeria to Morocco by a colonial officer and
ethnographer called Robert Montagne (1930) and used, with a few modifica-
tions, to explain politics in the High Atlas and southern Morocco. It has since
been adopted, in one form or another, by the majority of French and Moroccan
scholars (e.g., Berque 1955; Amahan 1998).

Here, as in Algeria, the central claim is that the key institution of political life is the council (*ljmā'*), which is supposed to exist at a number of different organizational levels, from extended family to village, then tribal fraction,
and finally tribe. Montagne insisted that the level of the tribal fraction (usually
comprising a few villages) was the principal one, but more recent scholars have
tended to focus on the village council. There has also been some debate about
who exactly attends such meetings, with responses ranging from all adult males,

---

5.   The Tashelhiyt term is rarely used in the region and almost entirely absent from the
      literature. I follow this general usage.

to one man per household, or just the principal village *notables*, depending on whom you ask. Such confusion notwithstanding, this vision of the Berber *res politica* has the signal advantage of offering an explanation of how cooperation is managed: through relatively open and equal, albeit highly gendered, debate, backed up by an institution endowed with the force of sanction. The model has also been enthusiastically taken up in development circles (e.g., Lacroix 2003; Lahoussain 2003), as its serendipitous conformity to the bureaucratic requirements of development agencies (many of which now make funding dependent on cooperation with a local institutional actor such as the "proto-democratic" village council) has endowed it with new vitality. It was, in any case, this sort of institution that I expected to find when I set out to conduct my doctoral research on interactions between the local political apparatus and imaginaries and those of the state.

THE HUNTING OF THE *LJMĀ*

> Just the place for a Snark! I have said it thrice:
> What I tell you three times is true.
> Lewis Carroll

I duly spent the first six months of my stay trying to attend the village council. I loitered outside the mosque or waited in the ablutions room while the rest of the village men listened to the weekly sermon and performed their prayers, but afterward, when they ought to have been conducting their meetings, they instead went home for couscous. And when I asked why there was no council, they looked puzzled and replied that perhaps there would be one next week, *in sha' allah*. And a few times there apparently were, but I only found out about them afterward and nobody was very keen to explain to me how things worked or how they were organized. I was, of course, inclined to attribute this to an understandable desire to keep the anthropologist, that "thief of knowledge" (see chapter 4), at arm's length, and there was doubtless something of this to it, but the longer I stayed and the more of these "councils" I eventually managed to attend, the clearer it became that something more was at play. Men[6] certainly

---

6.   The *ljmā'* is a male-only gathering, although in the village where I worked, a female *ljmā'* was once organized to discuss the possibility of developing a weaving

did meet up to discuss important events and when they did so, they sometimes referred to such gatherings as *ljmā't* (although it was far more common simply to say *njmā'*—we gathered), but these events did not quite tally with the formal meetings described in the literature.

For a start, they could be held almost anywhere: on the roof of the mosque; in the guest room of one of the senior families; in a field; by the river; wherever, in fact, was most appropriate. Nor were there strict, recognized rules of attendance. If I asked, people might say that it was one man per household, but some of the larger households sent several representatives and some sent none at all. Other times, they said that all adult males were attending, but many failed to show. There were also smaller meetings, *en petit comité*, which might bring together the so-called *sab'a n ikhfawn* (the "seven heads" of the most significant village families), but often there were not seven of them; the name did not correspond to any sociological reality and was more of a shorthand for when the wealthy gathered. And sometimes meetings could bring together people from several villages, although here again, it was never clear who was supposed to be attending. Nor was there much in the way of protocol or procedure: in principle, everybody has the right to speak and none can silence another, but there was no fixed order, no real chair, though some men did try to guide the debate. So participants might speak all at once, shouting over each other; some leapt to their feet and demanded to be heard, threatening to leave if they were not listened to; arguments broke out in different parts of the room, sometimes spilling over into the corridor.

Now these meetings I witnessed were recognizably cut from the same ethnographic cloth as the classic descriptions of the *ljmā'*: we see what look like councils of notables, village councils, and even supra-village councils; they resolved problems, made decisions, raised money and organized "statute labor" for collective projects, and then implemented them. What they lacked, however, was the formal, statutory quality of full institutions. When Montagne, say, discusses lineage, village, and sub-fractional councils, he speaks of them as if they were the predictable, institutional expressions of recognized organizational levels of society. So, if we have a problem that concerns the village, then we summon the village council, and if we have a higher-level issue then we transition to the sub-fractional council. In each case, there are implicit rules of attendance,

---

cooperative. The project came to naught, but the idea that women could gather, though funny, was not unthinkable.

composition, and procedure. It is simply a matter of *invoking the rule*, where a rule is understood in the broadly Wittgensteinian sense of a prescriptive convention that must be performatively enacted by the people who follow it.[7] And it is, I suggest, in this idea of the invocation or instantiation of a rule that full institutionality consists. The French anthropologist, Marc Abelès, for instance, argues that institutions are characterized by a necessary duality or tension, found in the opposition between "the process that leads to the production of [constitutive] rules" and "the resulting organization" (1995: 73). The institution, then, exists in this conceptual and perpetual to-ing and fro-ing between two states of existence: abstract and instantiated. And it was precisely this kind of predictable invocation of meetings from a recognized template that I did *not* find.

Instead the composition, form, and conduct of meetings were tailored to suit events and the inclinations of those who attend them. A couple of examples will give some idea of this process.

The water wars

In 2001, an inhabitant of the village of Alili, on the opposite side of the valley from Tiflilist, decided to dam an unused high mountain spring and use it to irrigate a tiny plot of land. No sooner had he done so, than a resident of Tiflilist upped and claimed that the spring belonged to him. There was a stand-off and neither side gave way; worse, the title deeds were unclear and both men considered themselves in the right. Considerable attempts at mediation were apparently undertaken.[8] Various configurations of notables, including the "seven heads," met up and councils bringing together the whole of both villages were also organized, but these failed to resolve the situation. Things dragged on for a year or so and finally both parties decided to take the case to court in distant Marrakesh—a truly remarkable decision for a group of men many of whom had vanishingly little Arabic and no direct experience of the legal system. And also a very expensive one in terms of the bribes required to pursue such a case; as one friend of mine put it: "ran ad

---

7. See the *Philosophical investigations*, Part I: 81–2 for a fuller discussion of the problem of how to conceptualize a rule.

8. I first visited the area in 2003 and so was not party to these initial events. The conflict was, however, ongoing for the whole of my seventeen-month stay in the village.

ffin kullshi iqariden g-lajwab n ibugaden arrig-tn s̲h̲an kullu-tn" *(they'll just pour the money into the lawyers' pockets until they've entirely devoured them [the litigants]). And so each side began to organize meetings (*ljmāʿat*) in order to raise the necessary funds and decide how to pursue the action.*

Alili is a small village composed of only two extended families, the men of which rallied round the owner of the land. Tiflilist, however, is much larger, more fractious and correspondingly harder to mobilize. On top of this, the owner of the stream was not in especially good standing among his lineage, who declined to support him. And so he turned to his friends. Luckily for him, he was a senior member of a group of men known as Ayt Aḥwash *(the party people) responsible for providing music for weddings and village festivities. The* Ayt Aḥwash *are a corporation of sorts, who are accustomed to raising funds for collective activity,*[9] *and it was they who formed the* ljmāʿ *to fight his cause. Each side continued to meet up (*jmāʿn*) on a regular basis for several years, as the case dragged on in the Marrakshi courts, but ultimately my friend's words proved prescient and the bribes too much for them. The case ground to a halt, the two parties ceased meeting up, and the incident continued to rankle: fifteen years later, there is still a palpable tension between the two parties.*

Exiling the "donkey"

This second case was sparked off by a conversation between a local school teacher (originally from the plains) and a tourist. A wedding was under way and the teacher, who was the only competent French speaker in the village, had accompanied her to the evening's festivities, put on by the Ayt Aḥwash*. There he tried, or so he subsequently claimed, to explain the subtle regional variations in dancing styles. Unfortunately, he was overheard by the only other person in the village with even a smattering of French (a young man raised in Casablanca, but back for the summer holidays), who came away with the impression that the teacher was comparing the locals to savages because they did not dance in male–female pairs, but in opposing rows of men and women. The young man duly reported the slur to all and sundry. The insult festered for a week or two and then erupted one*

9.   For a more ample discussion of the significance of such groups for Ishelhiyn ritual life, see Hammoudi's book-length discussion of the ritual masquerades they traditionally performed on a yearly basis, *La victime et ses masques* (1988).

day as the teacher was walking past the village shops. A group of young men called out "donkey" *and* "we'll eat your mother," *both fairly serious insults. Outraged beyond forbearance, the teacher span around, made a* bras d'honneur *and reportedly said* "You can take it like that … you and your whole tribe." *The young men responded by threatening him and he left the village the next morning to take the matter to the* caïd *(a military officer in charge of keeping the peace).*

This situation was a problem for the school administration and so the regional director, who spent most of his time in a nearby town, made a rare visit to Tiflilist, accompanied by the offending teacher. They arrived just as another wedding party was in full swing. An ljmā' *needed to be held, but most of the village men were engaged in the festivities, and so the decision was made to meet in the house of the bride and groom. A large room was commandeered for the purposes: on one side of the room sat the director, flanked by the remaining teachers from the village school, and on the other a constantly shifting array of village men who flitted back and forth between the ongoing party outside and the meeting within. Proceedings were fairly chaotic and the meeting dragged on for three hours, until the assembled company finally decided that they needed the room to feed the guests and it was best for the teacher to move to another village, some four kilometers away. He was no longer welcome in Tiflilist.*

What both these cases illustrate is how the shape and practice of the council is largely decided not by institutional charter, but by a combination of the event that calls it into being and existing patterns of social relations. So, in the first of the two examples above, the "Water Wars," we see councils being created from a range of different social materials: from ties of shared wealth (when the village notables meet), shared residence (whole villages), shared blood (one or more lineages) or even shared interests (the musicians). And the same term (*ljmā'*) can be used to describe all the different formats; none is semantically privileged. What is critical is that these council forms did not already exist in abstract form, ready to be implemented, but were conjured up in response to the problem. Similarly, where they are held and how they are organized is also, as we see in the second case, a fundamentally *ad hoc* process. The council simply crystallizes out of prevailing patterns of social relations as a response to the catalytic effect of an event. It can then retain the particular form it takes—with the same configuration of people coming together—so long as the problem or project remains, but once the situation is resolved, it dissolves back into the magmatic social material from which it came. The *ljmā'* is thus not one institution (or even several institutions) that persists over time, but at best a series of different institutions. This is quite clear in the example of the council of the Ayt Aḥwash, where they continued to meet as a "council" so long as the court case dragged on, but once it was over, they went back to making music. Equally, when the village built the twenty kilometer track that led to the metaled government road, carving it out of the cliff-face with dynamite and pick-axes, they met with a cobbled together coalition of villages from two different sub-fractions to raise money and organize labor. And they continued to meet in this form until the job was done. But they have never met since. Events have not called for it.

I have suggested elsewhere (Carey 2007) that these councils are best thought of as "ephemeral institutions," destined like the mayfly to die with the day, but it would not be outlandish to argue that the *ljmā'* is not really an institution at all. In many ways it is more like a political technology or mode of sociality that can be adapted to the situation at hand. Were we to liken it to classical Greek political practice, then it is less the formal *ecclesia* and more the informal *syllogos*—a simple gathering, lacking explicit protocol or powers and that works indirectly.[10] Either way, and here I shall stick to the term institution, what matters is that the *ljmā'* has no durability, no ability to project itself through time. And it is the proximity of its temporal horizon that militates against the possibility of coercion and so makes it truly anarchic. This point is critical: *coercion, once it moves beyond direct physical compulsion, can be thought of as a function less of brute force than of temporal extensibility.* One notable expression of this line of thought is Woodburn's classic (1982) distinction between immediate-return and delayed-return systems of production and consumption in hunter-gatherer society. In immediate-return systems, people possess virtually nothing that they cannot fabricate in a matter of hours, and directly consume or make use of the fruits of their labor. Such societies, he argues, are characterized by fluid social organization, free choice of association, radical egalitarianism, and a total lack of dependency on others. The immediacy of the temporal horizon means that nobody has the wherewithal to coerce another, because she can simply up sticks and leave with little or no cost. In delayed-return hunter-gatherer systems, in contrast, people possess assets that require considerable temporal investment: for instance, boats, stockades, or storage facilities. These societies are markedly

10. Cf. Gottesman (2014: 199), who challenges traditional translations of *syllogos* as "nocturnal council" and suggests that it should rather be seen as an informal gathering, closer to a "salon" than a council proper.

less egalitarian; they generate dependency and require long-term commitment; in so doing, they make coercion possible.

Now there are vanishingly few immediate-return societies still in existence and the Ishelhiyn of the High Atlas certainly do not number among them, but the same principle applies, *mutatis mutandis*, to complex political systems. The greater the degree to which political institutions can project themselves over time, the greater their potential capacity for coercion. For example, I described the Kabyle village council, which served as a model for theories of political organization in the Moroccan High Atlas, as a "fully-fledged and coercive political institution": attendance is compulsory for all village men and fines are issued to absentees. Collection is enforced through control of the village cemetery: if you fail to pay your dues, then you can ultimately be denied the right to a burial in your natal village (Judith Scheele, pers. comm.). This is very clearly a matter of temporal projection, not just in the straightforward sense that failure to comply in the here and now carries an onerous long-term cost, but also in institutional terms, because the council that denies the right to burial in the here-and-now does so because it recognizes *itself* and its own legitimacy in the council that previously imposed the unpaid fine. It is the temporal continuity of the institutional form that makes this possible.

This marks a sharp contrast with the High Atlas *ljmā'*. When collective labor details are organized, attendance is ideally compulsory and when I asked what would happen if people failed to show, I was often told that they would have to pay *lhaqq* (literally "truth," "reality," or "justice," but here used to signify "reparation"). In practice, however, there was simply no way of enforcing this. I recall participating in a collective labor duty to clear the snow from the village road. I turned up on the first day and fewer than a fifth of village households had managed to send a laborer. We went home, held an *ljmā'* in the mosque and arranged to meet the next day. Attendance was scarcely any more impressive, but the road needed clearing and so we toiled all day in the wind and snow. No fines were issued or collected. Nor, to the best of my knowledge, were they issued on any other occasion and I cannot remember attending a work detail from which somebody was not absent. In one case, a young man from a relatively significant family even borrowed a large sum of money, left over from a collective engagement, from "the rest of the village." He never paid it back and no concrete steps were ever taken to recover it, even though it was the source of a great deal of resentment. Nor did it stop him from playing a major role in several future councils involved in managing projects funded by European NGOs.

The problem in recovering debts or issuing fines, despite people's assurance that they will do so, is not one of brute physical coercion. People could simply gather, march to a man's house and seize his livestock, as they sometimes claim they might. Rather, the problem is one of institutional continuity. Monies cannot be recovered because each council is a different entity and neither recognizes itself in previous instantiations of the council form nor is mandated to act as a projection of them. The will to impose fines and recover debts is present, the necessary institutional technology is not. When I first began to reflect on these questions, I imagined that the absence of such continuity, the absence of the durable institutions present in, say, Kabylia, was the result of the increased state presence and the gradual deliquescence of the indigenous institutional landscape—a familiar pattern from much literature on the evolution of "traditional" institutions of governance under colonialism. Now state institutions may have been a marginal presence in the area where I worked (see chapter 4), but as the previous examples show, the state was still an extremely significant and forceful, albeit peripheral, coercive presence. And this, my thinking went, might have sufficed to strip local institutions of their purpose, form, and temporal continuity.

But there is, in fact, good reason to suppose this not be so. The area was only colonized in the 1930s and until at least the 1960s, the state was still effectively four days' walk away. I spent a great deal of time talking to people who remembered those times and I never got the sense that it had been very different. They did not reminisce about the durable and effective institutions of their youth. Indeed, the more rigid councils of Kabylia might in fact be the product of a much longer colonial history (François Pouillon, pers. comm.) and it seems that the massively increased presence of NGOs in the High Atlas might be leading to a similar evolution in local institutions. Time will tell. For now, the question that remains is: what prevents the sedimentation of durable, and so coercive, institutions?

ACCIDENTAL ANARCHISTS

In the ethnographic anarchist literature, the answer to this question is invariably that the institutions of anarchy are chosen. The classic example of this deliberate choice of "powerless" institutions is Clastres' discussion of Amerindian chiefs (1962). Clastres begins by establishing a broad opposition between the hierarchical societies of the Andean cordillera and the more egalitarian societies of lowland South America, where political organization is characterized by chiefs whose most remarkable trait is their "almost complete absence of authority" (1962: 52). Instead, Clastres maintains, they live in a gilded cage. The chief is usually granted the (often exclusive) right to take several wives, but with this come obligations: to give freely of his property and of his oratory.[11] Chiefs are frequently forced to work unusually hard in order to maintain a supply of gifts to their subjects and, in many Amerindian societies, they are obliged to give a daily exhortatory speech at dawn or dusk, but—and this is crucial—their words have no force of law and even, he suggests, no meaning as such: they are not a right, but a duty and the obligation to speak transforms words into mere empty vessels. In short, the supposed institution of power is devoid of power.[12]

For Clastres, the existence of such institutions can only be a choice: we cannot admit that "the effective *outcome* of the operation (the lack of authority of positions of power) is merely contingent to the initial *intention* (the promotion of the political sphere)" (1962: 62, original emphasis) and this for two reasons: first, because such institutions are so widespread[13] and it is too much of a coincidence to suppose that the same accident repeated itself across an entire continent;[14] and second, because to suggest that anarchic institutions are accidental would be to deny "primitive people" creativity, to suggest that they had no part in producing their own political systems. Rather, he argues that the powerless chief is the reasoned fruit of an "intuition that acts as a rule for them [these societies]: to wit, that power is essentially coercive" (1962: 64). He further

---

11. The obligation to distribute wealth and act as orators had been earlier identified, along with peacekeeping, as the essential characteristics of the North American "titular chief" (Lowie 1948); Clastres simply expands upon this concept.

12. As might be expected, this radical claim has not gone uncontested and certain authors have, for instance, argued that "Amerindian chiefs' speech has, through its aesthetic and moral dimension, a politically relevant role in the production of sociality" (Guerreiro 2015: 63). My point is not to enter into these debates, but merely to note that Clastres (along with many others) supposes the chief to have no direct power.

13. Descola (1988) strongly disputes this, contesting both Clastres' ethnographic claim that the Amerindian chief is universally powerless and the underlying image of lowland Latin America as composed of small-scale, fragmented and stateless societies; he draws on archaeological sources to suggest that this state of affairs is in fact a product of the colonial encounter, rather than of a fierce anti-state ideology.

14. Although if the initial conditions are similar, it is unclear why the same accidental result could not be supposed to repeat itself.

develops this idea in a later work where he contends that these societies should not be thought of as state*less*, but as societies *against* the state (1974). In other words, their members not only have an intuition that power is coercive, but even of where such coercion must ultimately lead—to the iniquity of the state form. They therefore design their political institutions in such a way as to neuter the very possibility of authority: "*the space of chieftanship is not a locus of power* and the (inaptly named) figure of the primitive "chief" in no sense prefigures that of the future despot" (1974: 175, original emphasis).

This same set of ideas—that people in anarchic societies have a sense of what coercive institutions must ultimately lead to and that the existence of powerless institutions cannot be contingent, but must be by design—is taken up time and again in the more recent literature. In his epic anarchist history of highland southeast Asia, *The art of not being governed* (2009), James Scott forcefully argues that the fluid social, economic, and political organization typical of the region is not simply the default Arcadian state of prestate societies, but has been "purposefully crafted both to thwart incorporation into nearby states and to minimize the likelihood that statelike concentrations of power will arise among them" (2009: 8). The inhabitants of Zomia are "maroons" (runaway slaves), who have fled the indentured existence of despotic plains states and sought their freedom in the hills. Almost every aspect of their existence, he contends, from the types of plants they cultivate to the widespread absence of literacy can be seen as a "more or less deliberate adaptation" (2009: 24) to life outside and against the state.

Graeber presents an even stronger version of this argument. He suggests that anarchistic societies see "greed and vainglory" as "moral dangers so dire [that] they end up organizing much of their social life around containing them" (2004: 24) and then proceeds to present the reader with a series of ethnographic examples that look much like the institutional landscape of the Moroccan High Atlas as I have described it. So the Tiv of Nigeria have "no political institutions larger than the compound" and consider "anything that even began to look like a political institution [... as] intrinsically suspect" (2004: 27), whilst in the rural Madagascan communities where he himself worked, "most local decisions were made by consensus by informal bodies, [and] leadership was looked on at best with suspicion" (2004: 28). What is important here is that he sees these institutions as an organizational counterpower that embodies an "alternative ethics" and seeks to transform the "internal tumult" of political existence into "those social states ... that society sees as the most desirable: conviviality, unanimity, fertility, beauty," etc. (2004: 35). Anarchic institutions are not only chosen as a bulwark against tyranny, but they also embody and strive toward a particular vision of the good—one that very often embraces ideals related to trust, such as conviviality and unanimity, and that very serendipitously seems to overlap with that of the anarchist anthropologist.

This, I would counter, is too univocal and too idealistic a vision of actual anarchism, at least as it is practiced in the High Atlas *ljmā'*. For a start, the people I spoke to about these councils unsurprisingly held a wide range of attitudes toward them. There was no clear alignment of opinion in favor of a supposed alternative political ethics; rather, they disagreed as vocally and heartily about the *ljmā'* as they did during it. Diversity of opinion is, of course, often a necessary casualty of sociological simplification, but here it is important, because for every villager who shared the Tiv's apparently unanimous suspicion of anything resembling a fully-fledged political institution, there were several others who lamented the absence of a tighter institutional framework. It is quite simply often inordinately difficult to get anything done in such a fragmentary institutional environment. As we saw above, the simple matter of clearing the road of snow can take several days to organize and this difficulty is multiplied for more complex undertakings: serious talks began as to how best to tap a distant spring to provide standing water for the village in 2004; in 2013, they were still ongoing. The fact that several villages managed to self-organize and build a road (an undertaking that took some two years) is testament not to the efficacy of their institutions, but to the desperate necessity of easier access to the plains. Many people see this not as the price of freedom, but as crippling limitations on their scope for action and openly call for institutions with more effective force of sanction.

In sum, the non-coercive nature of local political councils is not a matter of collective agreement, let alone design. Instead, we must look for the root causes of their ephemerality and consequent lack of coercion in something resembling the "suspicion of leadership" voiced by Graeber's Madagascan interlocutors. For if there is anywhere unanimity of opinion regarding the *ljmā'*, it lies in the belief that anybody who plays a significant role in the organization of any set of councils will necessarily make use of this position to further their own ends. Over the years, I have witnessed multiple projects in the area, including new bridges, new pathways, new school buildings, and a public bathhouse that never got built. Some of these were funded locally, some were projects brought in by international NGOs; all were attached in one way or another to some kind of ephemeral council body, which would often claim to foreign NGOs (and quite unbeknownst to the rest of the village) that it was the official council. And in every case, the people involved were widely accused, even by their close friends and family, of "eating" (_shan_) a good deal of the collective funds. The only people who ever denied this were the accused individuals themselves. In the local context, it would of course be unacceptable to speculate on people's motives for playing a central role in these projects (see chapter 1), but their supposed actions can, as I have argued, be read as a shorthand for motive. And it is understood that everybody, without exception, is untrustworthy—that they must be monitored or they will eat everything.

Such self-serving behavior may be tolerable in the short term and in pursuit of a clear, immediate goal, such as a new road, but in the long term it is unacceptable. This economic mistrust is further compounded by a political mistrust: that people will use their institutional position to exploit and lord it over others. This too is intolerable. And so once the immediate goal is achieved, people systematically withdraw from collective political activity. They drag their feet, fail to attend meetings and undermine the continuity of the endeavor. They deploy, to hark back to an idea developed by Scott in an earlier work, something resembling "weapons of the weak" (1987), but these weapons are not directed at the institution itself, or at the coercive potential it embodies; they are simply an expression of independence driven by a deep-seated mistrust of others. The ephemerality of institutions and their lack of coercion is an unintended consequence of these practices born of mistrust.

In saying this, I do not wish to deny that inhabitants of anarchist societies, like those of the Moroccan High Atlas, have a degree of creativity and agency in their own political destiny. The general political style of Atlassian politics, based on consensus, debate, fluidity, relative equality, and segmentation is, of course, of their own making. This does not, however, mean that the precise contours of their institutional environment are necessarily chosen. This is true in the general sense that institutions are often largely self-perpetuating: once we have produced them, they produce us in such a way as to ensure their continued existence. In his recent popular history of mankind, _Sapiens_, Harari makes the throwaway remark that "we did not domesticate wheat. It domesticated us" (2014: 81), as past a certain population density, humans' dependence on agriculture forces them to organize their societies around the cultivation of staple crops. Much the same point can be made regarding the state: past a certain degree of sociological complexity, we must organize our societies in such a way as to preserve it. Outside of revolutionary contexts, then, nobody chooses their political system. It is also true in the sense that political and sociological realities are, contrary to Clastres' energetic claim, always partially "contingent to… initial *intention[s]*." And they are contingent both because reality is unpredictable and because, as transactional anthropologists (e.g., Paine 1967) often reminded us, collective effects come from individual actions. At least in the High Atlas, it is the sum of multiple people's separate mistrust that produces anarchic institutions, not the unitary force of their collective desire for a better world.

AMORAL INSTITUTIONS

The unchosen and ultimately accidental nature of the council form is further reflected in its lack of ideological orientation. This is evident in two related ways: in the ends it seeks and in the style of argumentation deployed. Recall Graeber's bold assertion that organizational counterpower aims to produce "those social states … that society sees as the most desirable: conviviality, unanimity, fertility, beauty." This is simply an excessively meliorist example of an idea that runs like a thread through Western political thought, stretching back to Aristotle's claim in *The politics* that the ultimate end of the political community (the city) is, in Agamben's particular translation, "life according to the good" (*il vivere secondo il bene*).[15] In other words, politics and political institutions are, for both theorists and practitioners alike, concerned not merely with the mundanities of existence, but also with the attainment of certain abstract ideals.

This, I think, is not really how people in the High Atlas consider their *ljmā'at*. In all the many conversations I had about local political practice, I cannot recall an instance when somebody said to me that the aim of a *ljmā'* or indeed of *ljmā'at* in general was anything other than a practical one. The purpose of a meeting might be to smooth over a problem, "align our speech" (*isgem wawal*), build a bridge, or expel a teacher, but it was not in abstract terms to improve existence or make life in general better. Just as the *ljmā'*, qua political technology, is not the expression of a shared ideological commitment, no more does it strive toward abstract ideological goals. This specific orientation towards the concrete is, I suggest, in large part a product of its ephemerality. As the council is not

---

15. The passage can be found on pages 58 and 59 of Jowett's translation of *Politics* (1999). Agamben's translation is on page 4 of *Homo Sacer* (1995).

convened, but each time created anew and in response to a particular event, its orientation is a function of that event. Ideology does not have time to sediment itself. Simply put, mistrust generates ephemerality and ephemerality imposes a systematic orientation toward the contingent.

This same absence of ideology is evident in the arguments deployed for and against particular projects or courses of action during these meetings and in political discussion more generally. These are, in my experience, largely limited to the implications and consequences of different courses of action and typically (although not invariably) eschew arguments by ideology, which appeal to religion, the good, progress and so forth. A particularly clear example of this was one meeting organized to debate the construction of a public bathhouse—the pet project of a French nurse who had worked in the village for a year and then independently raised the funds and returned to the area to carry it out.

The weight of public opinion was against the project, largely because the man who would have managed it was suspected of being a little too fond of power. This, though, was not a valid reason for rejecting the idea in a political forum and so people variously argued that there was insufficient water, that it would lead to women walking the streets of the village at night, that it would not be possible to arrange a system for the management of the bathhouse, and so forth. Those in favor (the French nurse and his friends) suggested that it would mean fewer people fell ill from infections and that it would be pleasant to be able to wash. Nobody, however, raised the importance of cleanliness in Islam, and the moral arguments in favor of hygiene typical of nineteenth-century Euro-American debates regarding public bathhouses were equally absent.[16] More telling still was the intervention of one young man, the first locally educated boy to attend university, as well as a scion of the village's leading family. His youth and status meant that people listened grudgingly but quietly while he reflected on the symbolic and material value of water and the question of progress (*ttqaddam*). Afterwards, though, everybody agreed that "he did not know how to speak" (*ur isin a isawl*). It was not the oratorical style that was amiss, but the style of argument—his appeal to abstract and so irrelevant notions of the good, such as progress. How though to explain this relative absence of argument by ideology?

Unlike in the case of the ends pursued by the *Ijmā'*, there is no particular reason for supposing that the ephemerality of the institution militates in and

---

16. See, for instance, Williams (1991: 25).

of itself against the deployment of ideological argument. Nor is it that such argument is unfamiliar in a local context. As mentioned in chapter 1, the village where I worked has a long history of sending its young men to religious seminaries in the south, and the wave of reformist dispute that has swept the Muslim world over the last fifty years has scarcely left the High Atlas untouched. Such theological debate is almost entirely concerned with appeals to abstract conceptions of the good.

Why then do they not bleed over into political argument? In an earlier work, I argued that the general exclusion of arguments by religion from the political sphere has something to do with their absolute and therefore potentially coercive quality (Carey 2013). If someone suggests that a particular course of action is imperative because religiously necessary, then it compels the listeners to acquiesce or imperil their reputation as a good Muslim. And local people cherish their autonomy and don't like being seen to be coerced—or indeed to coerce. This analysis is, up to a point, valid, but it is hard to extend it to arguments by the good more generally. It is unclear why an appeal to progress would be coercive. I can only suppose, therefore, that their exclusion has something to do with people's perception of the political sphere more generally. Perhaps it is that politics is simply not seen as a sphere for working towards the good. The ephemeral political institutions in which it is performed are not only the result of contingency, but are also always oriented toward the contingent and this defines the purview of politics.

CONCLUDING REMARKS

Having begun this chapter with a pair of assertions, I'd like to end it with a pair of reflections. The first is that once you strip anarchism of its ideological apparel—of its embedded anti-state intentionality and striving after the communal good—then it actually begins to look very much like another form of political practice born of radical mistrust: Realpolitik.[17] What they both share is an emphasis on the contingent aspects of existence at the expense of the ideal, on dealing with things as they are rather than as they ought to be. Lived anarchism,

---

17. There is a case for arguing that the father of Realpolitik, Ludwig von Rochau, in fact had a rather idealistic conception of his invention. I am using the term in the more disabused Anglo-Saxon sense.

in other words, is not some Pollyannaish utopianism, but a political practice born of unflinching pragmatism. The second relates to ideas of the good more generally. In a recent and influential article, Joel Robbins (2013) has argued for an anthropology focused on "the ways in which different societies strive to create the good in their lives" (2013: 457) and one that "does justice to the different ways people live for the good" (2013: 459). He presents this as a progressive development within anthropological thought that would complement and extend existing work on the "suffering subject." It is also an approach that sits very comfortably with the current trust literature. Luhmann, for instance, suggests that by trusting "the actor binds his future-in-the-present to his present-in-the-future. In this way he offers other people a determinate future, a common future" (1979: 20). Trust is a social technology that allows for concerted action toward shared and abstract forms of good.

What I hope to have shown over the course of this chapter is that we should we wary of too readily and too broadly applying such an approach within anthropology. Progressive it may well be, but as I have argued, it is also a direct extension of nearly 2,500 years of unbroken European political theory. Where politics is about trust, then it is surely also about shared visions of the good. But where it is a function of mistrust, then perhaps we need to question the longstanding idea of man as "born to life, but existing essentially with regard to the good life" (*Politics* 1252b) and remember that he also essentially exists with regard to the contingent.

CHAPTER 4

Conspiracy, witchcraft, and theft
Manifestations of the mistrusting imagination

The previous chapters have explored the implications of a pervasive climate of mistrust for various aspects of social existence, from language and communication, to friendship, kinship, and politics. This final chapter reverses the perspective and asks how the social and epistemological infrastructures of everyday life help shape and enable prevailing imaginaries of mistrust, directing them against particular enemies and imprinting them with a particular style. I compare contemporary urban Ukraine and the Moroccan High Atlas and suggest that their very different infrastructural environments provide fertile ground for the development of conspiracy theories, on the one hand, and ideas of witchcraft and especially the fear of theft, on the other. The complex logistical frameworks of bureaucracy which dominate the Ukrainian social landscape offer an ideal backdrop against which conspiratorial imaginaries of organized others can emerge and flourish. Similar conspiratorial manifestations of mistrust can be found in Morocco, but they are extremely marginal in the High Atlas, where the pervasive structures of bureaucracy are not locally seen as playing a determining social role. Instead, the intimate infrastructures of kinship, friendship, and co-residence favor different sets of fears—for instance, of betrayal by the familiar other that is the witch.

The witch is not, however, the only nor even the primary object of mistrust in the area. Despite their structural differences, what fears of conspiracy and witchcraft share is an aesthetic of revelation that seeks to uncover the hidden machinations (of cabals or covens) that both determine and imperil existence. I suggest that in a context where, as we have seen, opacity is valued and attempts to expose that which it conceals duly frowned upon, it stands to reason that the archetypal enemy be not some hidden other, but to the contrary a figure who pries and uncovers. That figure is the thief—a thief who targets not only goods and chattel, but more importantly knowledge of others. Here the danger lies precisely in the act of discovery or revelation that is seen as the remedy to conspiracy and witchcraft. I link this to ideas of privacy, inscrutability, and autonomy discussed in chapter 1 and suggest that this form of mistrust thrives in a context where the primary social infrastructure is one of distributed knowledge, a context familiar to many of us today.

ON KULIKOVO FIELD

In late April 2014, my then partner and I were in the Black Sea port of Odessa in southern Ukraine, a city we know well, having regularly visited and occasionally lived in it over the last ten years. Odessa is a place that prides itself on a long history of cosmopolitan promiscuity and a generalized ethos of tolerance towards others.[1] And despite the protests and conflict that had engulfed Kiev in 2013, not to mention the nascent civil war in the east of the country, the *laissez-faire* spirit of the place seemed in many respects to be holding up well. We visited the markets, met up with friends, and celebrated Orthodox Easter. Though there was an undercurrent of tension in the city, a fear of imported violence and a great deal of uncertainty about the future of Ukraine, it did not feel like a place about to erupt into overt and internecine conflict between the so-called pro-Russian and pro-Ukrainian camps.

We took a flat in the city center and spent much of our time wandering the streets. On one Sunday afternoon stroll, we chanced upon a pro-Russian demonstration coming up the main pedestrianized shopping street, Deribasovskaia, towards the cathedral square. We stopped to watch the action and, in local fashion, comment on it with other passers-by. Now Odessa is a proudly Russian-speaking city and one that has been at the forefront of various campaigns to

---

1.   See Humphrey (2010) and Humphrey and Skvirskaja (2012) for a comprehensive
      discussion of the history of Odessan cosmopolitanism.

prevent "Ukrainianization" (*ukrainizatsia*) of the country, but there seemed to be little public affection for the motley crew of malcontents that made up the demonstration. People marched with Russian flags, Soviet flags, flags astonishingly adorned with both the face of Stalin and the slogan "Holy Rus'" (*sviataia rus'*).[2] One man was even dressed in full East German military regalia and carried a flag of the German Democratic Republic. We laughed along with our fellow spectators, who supposed that half of them must have been bussed in from the provinces: *"as if we didn't have enough urban crackpots* (gorodskie sumashedshie) *of our own,"* one of them remarked. The only pall on this otherwise perfect scene of tolerant urban bonhomie in the face of marginal discourses of sectarian fanaticism was one older woman who stopped to admonish us, saying in a shrill tone: "You mustn't laugh! We must drive them out." She was perhaps a little afraid and a little more clear-sighted.

We also visited the trade union building on Kulikovo Field—a public park named after the decisive battle between the Russian principalities and the Golden Horde in 1380—where the pro-Russians (who were also referred to as separatists) had established their camp. In front of the building, right in the middle, was parked a military Jeep, draped in camouflage netting and adorned with the words "Odessa Mama," an expression used by people of all political stripes to indicate the strength of their attachment to the city (and one that is often seen printed on tourist merchandise). On either side of the Jeep were tent compounds, including one claiming to be a "people's cathedral" (*narodnyi sobor*), adorned with the slogan "Against the values of Euro-Sodom" (*protiv tsenosti evrosodoma*) and filled with photos of Berkut (Ukrainian special police) officers, fallen in the battle against the Euromaidan protestors in Kiev. Another displayed further invocations of Holy Rus', this time associated with the political and spiritual union of Russia, Belarus and Ukraine. And on the other side of the little square, in front of the building, were yet more tent compounds where disaffected middle-aged men performed military-style physical exercises in front of the occasional spectators. This slightly intimidating martial atmosphere was, however, undercut by the presence of mobile coffee vans, who had set up on the middle of the square to serve the onlookers to this bizarre scene. These people were not without support and they certainly tapped into a wellspring of local

---

2.   Rus' implicitly refers to Kievan Rus', an Eastern Slavic proto-state that existed from the ninth to the thirteenth century and which is seen as the predecessor of subsequent Slavic states in the region.

discontent, but they seemed more like a peculiar sideshow than a real threat to the peace.

I even attended, with some trepidation, a football match on Easter Sunday, along with some acquaintances: a retired university lecturer, a young internet entrepreneur, and a former sailor. I had expected to find a bastion of fierce regionalist spirit—the Odessan team is, after all, called *Chernomorets* (the "Black Sea-er")—and anti-Ukrainian sentiment. Nothing could have been further from the truth. The local "ultras," dressed in striped sailor tops, held up their scarves and sang along to the club anthem (*"Black Sea sun, Black Sea sky/ Chernomorets, o team of mine"*), cheering as patriotic images of Ukrainian landscapes flashed up on the huge screens and a Ukrainian flag fluttered over the endless steppe. The atmosphere was friendly and after an undeserved local victory over the visiting team from Dnepropetrovsk (just next to the eastern separatist regions), we spilled our way out of the stadium and streamed back to the city center, home and away fans mingling freely.

A week or so later, just two days after we had left Odessa, violence broke out. On May 2, in the early afternoon, fans of Chernomorets and Metalist Kharkiv gathered on the cathedral square to take part in a march for Ukrainian unity also attended by members of the neofascist and pro-Ukrainian "Right Sector" (*pravyi sektor*) movement. This was met by a counter-demonstration involving the activists from Kulikovo Field, led by a group known as the Odessan Brigade. The confrontation quickly escalated, with running skirmishes, exchanges of petrol bombs, and barricades built throughout the center. Around four o'clock, there were reports of firearms being used and a pro-Ukrainian activist, Igor Uganov, was shot in the street where we had been staying, apparently from behind police lines. Skirmishing continued, leaving a total of six dead and many more casualties. As the afternoon wore on, the pro-Russian demonstrators gradually retreated to Kulikovo Field. During this time, the match between Chernomorets and Metalist Kharkiv had kicked off, but news of the clashes quickly spread on social media and when the match finished, the fans left the stadium and marched on Kulikovo Field. Here things get hazy. What is known is that the pro-Russians were driven inside the trade union building, which they then barricaded; the tent compounds were set alight; there were further exchanges of petrol bombs; and then the trade union building caught fire on the second and third floors. Official reports state that forty-two people died in the resulting blaze.

A few days after these events, my partner received an email from an Odessan friend containing photographs, supposedly taken at the scene, of charred and sometimes bound bodies. The friend, a seemingly level-headed former journalist, said that it felt like living in a different world, that even if Putin sent in troops it would take days for them to reach the city. She added that there were credible rumors that the numbers of dead had been vastly understated. That anything up to four hundred people might in fact have died in the trade union building, that they had been shot, not burnt to death, and their bodies had been spirited away in the night. She was expecting the city to be occupied by troops from Kiev: so-called "punishment battalions" (*karateli*) sent to exact a toll on the local population for their insubordination.

The head of police, who was suspected of having helped Igor Uganov's killer to escape, had in fact already been replaced, as had the governor. But in the end, these predictions of imminent invasion were not borne out: neither Moscow nor Kiev occupied Odessa. The rumor-mill continued, though, to churn out stories of what had really happened that day on Kulikovo Field. Below, in no particular order, are some of the ideas put forward on various Ukrainian internet sites and social media:[3]

- ❖ There had in fact been no fire at all. It had been staged to look like a fire so as to cover up an extensive massacre inside.
- ❖ In any case, the firemen had come suspiciously late to the scene.
- ❖ Militarily trained elements of the neofascist Right Sector had been waiting inside the trade union building for the pro-Russian demonstrators.
- ❖ Some people had been seen on the roof of the building, which shouldn't have been possible as it was a national holiday and the employees with keys would all have been at home.
- ❖ It was a planned mass-murder of Odessans. Flammable stuff had been placed inside the building to help ignite the fire.
- ❖ Many of the pro-Russian demonstrators were not what they seemed, but agents of Kiev who had turned on the others once they had fled inside.
- ❖ Perhaps they were not agents of Kiev, but part of a Zionist-American false flag conspiracy.
- ❖ There were barricades set up inside to prevent the victims fleeing the fire; these could have been set up in advance by the Right Sector.

---

3. Some of the theories can be found (in Russian) on the following websites: http://frallik.livejournal.com/781599.html; http://vlad-dolohov.livejournal.com/876486.html; http://pangalushko.livejournal.com/556.html

❖ Some pictures showed a young man and woman who had not been burnt; instead, their necks had been broken. Only a professional could have done this.

❖ The assassins had stripped the dead of their clothes and disguised themselves so they could slip out unnoticed.

❖ In fact, most of the killings had been carried out in the basement, where women and children had been axed and clubbed to death.

❖ The marks on the bodies were not burns, but cyanosis caused by gas-poisoning. [As it transpired, even the local police declared over the next few days that chloroform and white phosphorous had been used in the building.]

❖ The bodies had been moved after death. The "junta" (i.e., Kiev) had sent a special group of agents provocateurs to the city pretending to be police reinforcements from a different region. It was they who had shot Igor Uganov, before infiltrating the trade union building and carrying out the massacre. They had moved some of the bodies to the basement, but when the fire broke out, their route to the basement was blocked and so they had placed the bodies in the flames to make it look as though they had burnt to death.

❖ Or, alternatively, the *agents provocateurs* were in fact FSB (Russian secret service) agents sent to destabilize the city and prepare it for the Russian invasion.

What first struck me about this rapid escalation of competing and contradictory theories was just how *socially* and *politically* committal they were. People might not have been committed to the content of the theories—indeed, those we spoke to seemed more inclined, in classic conspiratorial fashion, to doubt everything than to pin their colors to any particular interpretation—but the mere fact of mooting such ideas forced them to take sides in seemingly irreversible ways. Odessa, as mentioned, is a city that prides itself on its tolerance of diversity and long history of interethnic and interfaith coexistence. And such tolerance can surely survive tragic events such as those of Kulikovo Field, just as it survived pogroms in the late-nineteenth and early-twentieth centuries; but the proliferation of such extreme explanations of those events forced people to assume positions from which it seemed almost inconceivable to re-establish a peaceful *modus vivendi*, compelling people who had previously foregrounded their identity as Odessans to align themselves with either the pro-Russians or the pro-Ukrainians in new and uncompromising ways. This sense of irrevocability was further reinforced by the utter collapse of trust on all sides. To whom could they possibly turn for an impartial assessment of what had happened? The European Union? They would be dismissed as in league with the neofascists in Kiev. The United Nations? A puppet of the Zionist-American global hegemon. In short, this is a classic example of what numerous scholars have discussed elsewhere: the collapse of trust in institutions and the absence of an arbiter give free reign to the conspiratorial imagination (Giddens 1991; Latour 2004).

I was also struck, however, by the extraordinary logistical complexity of many of the theories put forward. Right Sector militants had passed themselves off as police units from elsewhere, infiltrated the trade union building, set up barricades and placed explosives unseen, faked a fire, infiltrated the pro-Russians, contrived to ensure that the same pro-Russians returned to and entered the desired building, infiltrated or otherwise hampered the fire service, killed hundreds of people without leaving witnesses, and spirited away the bodies in the dead of night despite the trade union building being the center of sustained media attention for the next few weeks. To have managed these things would have required not only extreme subterfuge, but above all a vast and complex organizational infrastructure—one that penetrated and gave shape to the social world in its entirety. And this sort of infrastructural complexity is, I suggest, in fact a consistent feature of conspiratorial thought.

Two months later, on July 16, when Malaysia Airlines Flight 17 from Amsterdam to Kuala Lumpur was shot down over eastern Ukraine killing all 298 people on board, many pro-Russians immediately and persistently claimed that the plane had been loaded with dead bodies and shot down by Americans to smear them. This idea was presumably borrowed from an episode of the BBC's Sherlock television program aired two years earlier and, just as in the program, it would have required a bureaucratic machine of unimaginable sophistication to pull it off. The same is true of the endless American conspiracies about the New World Order or the Zionist fantasies that plague the Middle East. They systematically bear the stamp of what I'm calling the bureaucratic imagination.

CONSPIRACY AND THE BUREAUCRATIC IMAGINATION

The literature on conspiracy thinking, both academic and popular, has flourished so dramatically over the last twenty years that it is hardly possible to give a comprehensive overview of the field; as Boltanski notes, the genre basically constitutes a discipline in its own right (2012: 273), and one that has already been mapped and surveyed from a variety of angles (Knight 2000; Parish and Parker 2001; Boltanski 2012). I have no such totalizing cartographic aspirations. Instead, I would simply like to flag a number of persistent themes that crop up in this literature and that perhaps give us an insight into the *aesthetics* of conspiracy as a structured field of representation—i.e., the ways in which it both presents itself and is represented. These can be grasped by exploring the responses offered to four basic questions: What distinguishes conspiracy theories? What gives rise to them? What do they do? And, most fundamentally for my argument here, in what manner or style do they do it?

The first question, that of definition, is both essential and intractable, for whilst everybody can agree that conspiracy (from the Latin *conspirare*—to breathe together) involves one or more people plotting in secret to achieve some end, it is far from clear what distinguishes the conspiratorial mindset, which sees Reds under every bed, from the simple and undeniable assertion that conspiracies do in fact exist. Why is it paranoid to suppose that Washington is controlled either by a Zionist Occupation Government (ZOG) or by lizards, but eminently reasonable to suggest that the failure to achieve global agreement on action against climate change is principally the result of the concerted and covert action of large companies who lobby or buy off elected representatives? Distinguishing between them is a surprisingly difficult task because, from a formal perspective, conspiracy theories look remarkably similar to competing explanations of the social world. Indeed, one of the points that is most frequently made by scholars is the extent to which conspiracy adopts the trappings of "accepted discourse" in order to acquire legitimacy. For instance, Hofstadter notes in his classic discussion of *The paranoid style in American politics*, first published in 1964, that paranoid thought is marked by the amassing of facts and appeal to rational discourse that makes the "curious leap" of imagination characteristic of conspiracy possible:[4] "the enemy ... may be the cosmopolitan intellectual, but the paranoid will outdo him in the apparatus of scholarship, even of pedantry" (2008 [1964]: 32).

Those scholars, typically philosophers and political scientists, who have addressed the question head-on have, as a result, often focused on the nature or quality of the reasoning involved, variously suggesting that conspiratorial reason is overly reliant on "errant data" (Keeley 1999), is typically unfalsifiable

---

4.   See Bajuk (1999: 280) for an exploration of this process of steady accumulation and sudden leap of faith in the context of ideas of a continuity between the parallel Yugoslav mafia economy and contemporary Slovenian economic elites.

(Barkun 2003: 7; Lewandowsky et al. 2013: 630), or is prone to confirmation bias (Leman and Cinnirella 2007). Social scientists, in contrast, have tended to stress that even at the level of reason there are no clear distinctions to be made (Pelkmans and Machold 2011). Instead, they have often followed Hofstadter in highlighting the extent to which conspiracy theories ape or mimic mainstream discourses, not only in their attention to detail, but even in terms of the forms of reasoning involved, which are frequently compared to those of academic discourse (e.g., Bajuk 1999) and even detective novels (Boltanski 2012). Indeed, Song (2012), following Bratich (2008) goes so far as to suggest that it is this very process of mimicry that defines conspiracy theories, which he sees as "simulacra" in the sense of Deleuze (1968).[5] More frequently, though, social scientists have looked at the second and third questions: what gives rise to conspiracy theories and what social or analytical work they *do* for their adherents.

Hofstadter suggests that some conspiracy theories are initially born of genuine grievances, but the question of whether or not they are founded is generally seen as very secondary to the context from which they emerge: that of a catastrophic loss of trust often associated with some or other aspect of modernity (cf. Giddens 1991). This is variously identified as the dissolution of social recognition (Featherstone 2001), a sense of disenfranchisement (Heins 2007: 797), alienation (James 2001: 64), or a collapse of collective ideologies. The loss of trust can also be generated by a particular context of conflict or political transformation (Silverstein 2002: 650) or a civilizational loss of influence as in the Middle East (Pipes 1997: 5) or the post-Soviet space (Oushakine 2009), leading to a hankering after some imagined lost order.

In other words, conspiracy theories are very often seen as coming from a space of perceived marginality—not only by social scientists seeking to identify the subject position of their adherents, but also by the adherents themselves: as Quinn notes, conspiracy theories are also a way for people to express their distinctiveness, their atypical clear-sightedness and the idea that they, at least, are not dupes (2001: 119). And this, in part, is what conspiracy theories are seen as *doing* for those who espouse them. They not only emerge from, but are also a response to, this position of marginality. They criticize the supposed truths of the mainstream order, providing people with a sense of control and allowing them

---

5.   The Deleuzian idea of the simulacrum borrows the Platonic conceit of a model that does not simply copy an original, but also serves as a challenge to it. It rebels against its patron.

to reassert the existence of a kind of order in the face of a sense of powerlessness (Parker 2001: 204).[6] Finally, they are also sometimes presented as opening up an emancipatory space for new voices (Dean 1998; Featherstone 2001: 32). This somehow sympathetic, or at least ambivalent, attitude towards conspiracy theorizing is rather prevalent in the social (as opposed to the political) sciences,[7] perhaps because we recognize something of ourselves in their style of thought.

This question of style has been central to studies of the genre since Hofstadter's founding work *The paranoid style in American politics*, and much of it has focused on the overlap between conspiracy theorists and social scientists.[8] Both they and we work with an "occult" style of reasoning that looks beneath surface appearances for hidden explanations; what Faubion (2001: 13) calls a "*sémiotique du soupçon*" or semiotics of suspicion.[9] This is an aesthetics of revelation and discovery that seeks to render the world transparent and that the Comaroffs trace back to the Enlightenment (2003: 291), but whose roots we might just as easily look for in the Inquisitorial idea that the truth of things is always hidden within and must be brought to the light.[10] But there is also, I suggest, another kind of

---

6.   It is worth noting that even when conspiracy theories are deployed by those in power (as with Nazi depictions of global Jewish cabals or Hutu denunciations of secret Tutsi attempts to seize power), they are typically presented as an alternative to mainstream ideas. This marginal or alternative quality is a necessary element of conspiratorial thought.

7.   Witness Marcus' collective volume, *Paranoia within reason* (1999), which essentially presents conspiracy theories as a form of liberating critique.

8.   As early as 1909, the French psychologists Sérieux and Capgras were drawing explicit parallels between people suffering from paranoid delusions and the newly emerging figure of the "sociologist": both were diagnosed as suffering from a form of "intellectual exaltation" and an "interpretative delirium or frenzy" (cited in Boltanski 2012: 248). And this comparison has since been made time and again: Latour remarks that conspiracy theories bear the "trademark" of "social critique" (2004: 230); Song recognizes in the conspiracy theorist a "begrudged long-lost brother" (2012: 11); and Soares suggests that "the rise of social science itself was based [like conspiracy] on the unveiling of the covert, the disclosure of deception, the revelation of what is hidden behind the masks of ideology" (1999: 225).

9.   This probably owes something to Sarraute's (1956) highly influential notion of the "era of suspicion"—i.e., the idea that literary modernity was characterized by the progressive development of a pervasive "mistrust" (common to both author and reader) of the characters in traditional psychological novels.

10. This is, of course, related to the confessional idea of truth production so thoroughly explored by Foucault (1976), though I would like to stress the Inquisitorial conceit that inner truth can be descried without the subject's willing participation.

aesthetic at play in conspiratorial thought; one that it does not necessarily share with the social sciences. That is an aesthetic of bureaucracy.

What we see, time and again, in such theories is that the shadowy forces pulling the strings backstage bear a curious resemblance to bureaucratic structures of various kinds. Here again, mimicry is the key characteristic of conspiratorial thought. From the underground Zionist global government that entrances and appalls the Arab Street to the satanic Vatican cabals that used to scare young Protestant children to sleep, by way of the secret masonic societies that so capture the European imagination (secret societies that, when they exist, conceive of themselves in explicitly bureaucratic terms),[11] the shape taken by the supposed conspiracy espouses or mimics the bureaucratic form that regiments the theorists' lives. It is perhaps no coincidence that conspiracy theories first emerge in recognizable form around the time of the French Revolution (Hofstadter 2008 [1964]), shortly after the term "bureaucracy" was invented to reflect the changing realities of administration (cf. Albrow 1970), that they wax over the next two centuries as bureaucracies play an ever increasing role in people's lives, and that they reach their zenith in those parts of the world where daily existence is, or has been, most clearly structured by the bureaucratic machine: the former Soviet space (Grant 1999), Turkey (Bulut 2005), or countries such as Syria (Reedy 2007; Rabo 2014) or Algeria (Silverstein 2002).

It is even tempting to suggest that the particular form that different conspiracies take is a reflection of the different bureaucratic regimes their theorists experience: so French conspiracy theorists might see the state everywhere (cf. Quinn 2001), whilst their English counterparts look for shadowy cabals that mirror the networks of private schools and Oxbridge colleges that provide their elites. Such oppositions are, however, too crude. Conspiracy theories have always migrated, ever since Augustin Barruel first laid the blame for the French Revolution at the door of the Bavarian Illuminati in 1797–98 and so set in train two hundred years of increasingly febrile global speculation. Nonetheless, it is interesting to explore which kind of conspiracies stick where. Hofstadter, for instance, remarks in passing that "the country is [allegedly] infused with a network of Communist agents, just as in the old days it was infiltrated by Jesuit

---

11. American co-masons, for instance, claim to have established a masonic "government of the craft," which they describe as "that bureaucracy which Freemasonry needs to ensure the continued functionality and expansion of the Order" (http://www.co-masonry.org/site/english/Government.aspx).

agents" (2012 [1964]: 26), thus reflecting not only a shift in the perception of the enemy (first Papists, then Socialists), but also I would argue in the style of bureaucracy, from the parastatal proto-bureaucracy of the church (the Jesuits are often seen as a prime mover in the expansion and establishment of Latin American bureaucracy [e.g., Wilde 2009]) to the fully-fledged Kafkaesque machine of state socialism. More interesting still, however, is the question of what form the mistrusting imagination takes in places where bureaucracy is not the only or even the principal infrastructure that shapes social existence.

INFRASTRUCTURES OF INTIMACY

In 2002, I was studying at an Arabic language school in the old imperial city of Fez, in central Morocco, and staying with a family who lived right in the heart of the medina, in a splendid stuccoed house built around a central courtyard. The family had fallen on hard times and was reduced to taking on foreign language students to supplement their income. On the day of my arrival, the eldest son sat me down and served me tea. He then proceeded to make small talk. Having first established that I came from the countryside, had a great many brothers and sisters, and didn't particularly support any football team, his mind quickly turned to Princess Diana of Wales—still apparently a hot topic some five years after her death in a car crash in Paris. He began by asking me if I knew who had killed her. I was new to the wider Middle East and innocently replied that I did not. It turned out to have been the Jews. And did I know why they had killed her? Again I drew a blank. He explained that it was to prevent an Arab and a Muslim becoming King of England. I shook my head. Dodi [Fayed— Princess Diana's then boyfriend, who also died in the crash] would never have become King. Why not? And so, slightly surprised at finding myself explaining the principles of hereditary monarchy to a man who lived in one, I said that as Diana was not herself heir to the throne, Dodi could not ascend to it, and even if she had been, he could only have been prince consort. My interlocutor mulled this over for a while and asked: "So why did the Jews kill her?"

I was to encounter similar conspiratorial claims time and again over the coming years, in Marrakech, Rabat, and Agadir, although most of the people who focused on the Diana case had a slightly firmer grasp of the subtleties of succession and so contended that the Jews had killed her to prevent the future King of England (William III) from having a Muslim stepfather. And more recently, I have come across such ideas in the High Atlas as well. In Spring 2016, I was talking with two young men from my extended family and the conversation drifted, for obvious reasons, to DAESH (Islamic State of Iraq and the Levant) and the conflagration that is at the time of writing engulfing the Middle East almost in its entirety. One of them suggested, in an offhand and rather non-committal way, that DAESH was funded by the West, which was simply continuing its decades-long practice of destabilizing the region in the pursuit of lower oil prices. I replied that whilst that line of reasoning was pretty understandable and whilst I agreed that the West had, by invading and then desolating Iraq, created the conditions in which a group like DAESH could emerge and flourish, I didn't think "we" were directly funding them. The financial backing, I continued, seemed to come largely from Saudi Arabia and oil revenues, and the idea that the West was deliberately keeping them afloat was, you know… and I fished around for a way to say conspiracy theory in Tashelhiyt or Arabic. My young friends helped me out and, in the process, offered up the further idea that 'Abu Bakr al-Baghdadi (the leader of DAESH) was actually a Jew, because his surname was toponymic—i.e., it means "of Baghdad."[12]

The interesting thing here was not the theories themselves, which were rather banal in a Middle Eastern context, but the fact that in the thirteen years I have been living in and visiting this part of the High Atlas, this was the very first time I had met with the sort of conspiratorial thinking that has so long been part of the discursive regime of the surrounding plains. This raises two immediate questions: why had I not encountered them before? And why was I doing so now? The answer to the first is, I suggest, that the High Atlas as I encountered it in the early 2000s was a place where the infrastructure of bureaucracy was still sufficiently shaky and distant that conspiracy theories simply lacked purchase. They had no place in the local conceptual landscape of mistrust. Morocco may be a typical French postcolony in which the bureaucratic machine is the principal mode of social advancement, but this is not so in the uttermost rural hinterlands.

---

12. This, I suspect, is a classic example of the migratory nature of conspiratorial thought. In a European context, toponymic names, such as Berlin, are indeed reliable indicators of Jewish forebears; in a Middle Eastern context, however, where toponymic surnames are incredibly common (cf. Geertz et al. [1979] on Arabic *nisba* name formation), they only clearly indicate Jewish ancestry if they are Spanish toponyms, such as Navarro or Toldano.

When I first settled in the mountains in 2003, there was one school in the surrounding twenty villages. The villagers had built it themselves and so far nobody had graduated from it. Accordingly, the only locals who had a foothold on the vast edifice of Moroccan bureaucracy were local elected representatives, of which there had so far been two. Most locals had only received a national identity card in the early 1990s, when they had chosen their surnames (a process that merits closer attention) and many older women and younger children were still bureaucratically invisible. Only one person from the area had migrated abroad; nobody else had left the country; and nobody was in registered employment. This is not to suggest that they lived somehow outside the state, but that the state was not primarily experienced via its apparatus as a complex infrastructure. Instead, for most people, it was embodied in the authoritarian person of the local *caïd*: a military figure whose principal task is to maintain order in the region and prevent sedition and who is but a paler instantiation of the personified might of the King. The state was not an infernal machine, but a hegemon. This is stony soil indeed for conspiracy theories—i.e., narratives of mistrust that, I have argued, draw on a bureaucratic imaginary to ensure their plausibility: why should people fear the secret machinations of covert societies and their diabolical logistical capabilities when they do not directly experience them as shaping their everyday lives?

This stony soil is in the process of transforming into more fertile ground for conspiracy as the state draws ever closer and assumes a more quotidian, structuring role. A new metaled road was completed in 2015 and with it came more regular visits from officialdom; livestock are now tagged and registered as part of the national herd; electricity has also arrived and with it bills that must, for the first time, be paid. Most significantly, all villages now have a school. The two young men I was speaking to were the very first generation to complete their primary education and attend the high school in the plains; one of them was the first locally-educated villager to graduate from university in Marrakesh, now looking for a job as a civil servant; and both had lived in the city for the last five years. It was no surprise that they had picked up conspiracy theories and, just as importantly, had a feel for their bureaucratic aesthetic. For most local people, however, raised outside the bureaucratic form and for whom it is still a marginal presence, this is not yet the case.

Instead, everyday life in the area is, as we saw in chapter 2, largely given form by the ramifying networks of kinship, affinity, and friendship. It is these networks and one's ability to draw on and make use of them that are locally seen as determining one's life chances, in much the same way as bureaucracy does in the plains.[13] Older brothers, like the biblical Cain, are destined (if they choose) to work the land and occupy the family in the village; their younger siblings, like Abel, are relegated to the alternately frigid and torrid mountainside, where they face the unenvied daily toil of taking the flock to pasture and retire, come evening, to frugal dinners in the Spartan comfort of a shepherd's bothy.[14] Economic and social differentiation along lineage lines means that people born into certain extended families were not only much wealthier, but until the arrival of the state school, were vastly more likely to receive a traditional Islamic education and so occupy a privileged social position. These extended kin ties also influence marital outcomes, trading partnerships, and the possibility of economic advancement. In short, the infrastructures of daily existence are *intimate* ones and the types of mistrust and images of the enemy that flourish in these intimate environments are quite different to the organized, logistical other of bureaucracy.

In a recent book, Peter Geschiere has argued that witchcraft always "conjures up the danger of attacks from close by [...] warning that seeds of destruction are hidden inside social relations as such" (2013: xv). Unlike conspiracy, whose enemy is the "other" (the Jew, the mason, the Catholic, the lizard race) and borrows the bureaucratic form in which it is embedded, witchcraft speaks a language of intimacy and betrayal.[15] The enemy is "one of us," not just superficially, but essentially. The danger lies in similarity and proximity, rather than in difference; in intimate embodied relations, rather than in the depersonalized forms of bureaucracy. Geschiere proceeds to chart the shifting contours of witchcraft in Cameroon over the last forty years, marking out a

---

13. The opposition between these two forms of social advancement, as well as the different techniques and strategies used to "mak[e] networks proliferate and hybridize" is one I have discussed at length elsewhere (Carey 2012: 195).

14. The pastoral idyll, and accompanying aesthetic, so central to European representations of shepherding, has no equivalent in the context of the High Atlas. Nobody waxes lyrical about spending their days trudging up and down mountains with only sheep for company.

15. This rapprochement of conspiracy and witchcraft is a common one. Faubion, for instance, describes them as "heuristic analogues" that feed off "semiotic indeterminacy," and nor are such ideas restricted to academia: as an anonymous Cameroonian attendee of a talk by Peter Geschiere put it: "When will you Europeans stop exporting your forms of sorcellerie to Africa: Freemasonry, Rosicrucianism, and homosexuality?" (2013: 1).

three-fold progression from the 1970s to the present day. In the early 1970s, he describes an isolated rural world marked by an ideology of egalitarianism in which the newly emerging class of rural civil servants (*les évolués*) lived under constant threat of bewitchment by jealous relatives. Only relocation to a city could sever these dangerous ties of kinship. By the 1990s, the village and the city are no longer distinct worlds, but tightly bound together both by administrative structures and migrant labor. Witchcraft can reach clean across the country, but it is still kin who must be feared. Finally, Geschiere discusses the changes wrought by globalization and the new wave of migration to Europe. These migrant have families back home, who have often invested heavily in the adventure and strive to bind the distant migrant (a potential source of wealth) and ensure that he does not forget them. What Geschiere adroitly demonstrates with this string of examples spanning nearly half a century is that witchcraft in a Cameroonian context is always bound up with the intimate ties of kinship.

Intimacy, for Geschiere, is the central term of the witching imaginary, but whilst he claims that African witchcraft is best understood as the "dark side of kinship" (2013: 14), he also recognizes that intimacy can take other forms. This is drawn out in the extended contrast with European witchcraft in the 1970s as described by Jeanne Favret-Saada for a region of rural northwest France she calls the Bocage. Over a number of works (1977; 1981 [with Contreras]; 2015 [2009]), Favret-Saada depicts a world of small agricultural holdings based around the nuclear family unit and analyses witchcraft accusations as a form of therapy that allows for the strengthening of this unit by directing its potential for symbolic violence against a neighbor. She notes that not just any neighbor will do; the alleged witch must always be somebody with whom one has an "intimate" (*investie*) relation: "a best friend is a credible suspect" (2015: 73). For Favret-Saada, these accusations are best seen as a form of misdirection designed to draw attention away from tensions within the family (2015: 74). But one might just as well argue that they reflect the prevailing imaginary of intimacy. Favret-Saada describes a world in which relations of kinship are very often a matter of *haines de famille* or, "family hatreds" (2015: 74). Siblings disinherited by the unofficial practice of primogeniture must move away and so the nuclear family is left, as she notes, alone—isolated and indeed nucleated. Farmers and their families come then to rely on neighbors for company and support, both material and social. It is neighbors they see on their weekly trips into town and neighborly ties that constitute the infrastructure of social

existence. And so it is within this infrastructure that fear of betrayal and paranoia proliferate, just as in Cameroon they thrive in the imaginary infrastructure of kinship. What is significant is that in both cases, mistrust espouses the
contours of intimacy because it is intimacy qua infrastructure that shapes and
gives form to people's existence—and so betrayal, when it comes, comes from
within.

It is, then, unsurprising to find ideas and accusations of witchcraft in the
intimate social environment of the Moroccan High Atlas. Magic is, in any case,
officially recognized in Islam. The Qur'an speaks of witches as "those who blow
on knots" (113: 4) and al-Qarafi, one of the great scholars of the Maliki school
of Sunni Islam, dominant in Morocco, also recognized the existence of magic
and its capacity to alter the personality and behavior of its victims (*Al-Furuq*,
Vol. 4: 149).[16] Such ideas are present throughout contemporary Morocco. Radi,
for instance, notes that magic (*shur*) is typically used to harm the victim or "to
obtain something from him against his will. It is supposed to provoke altered
physical or psychological states" (2013: 72). She remarks that just as in sub-
Saharan Africa and Europe, it is directed towards intimates: family, neighbors,
friends, colleagues, etc. (Radi 2013). It is also widely understood as divisible into
a number of different types, such as separation magic, love magic, hallucina-
tory magic, stultifying magic, maddening magic, bleeding magic, and sickening
magic (2013: 76).

Of these numerous types, the two most prominent in the High Atlas are,
in my experience, separation magic and love magic. I recall once finding grains
scattered in front of my threshold and a friend suggesting that it was somebody
trying to sever our relationship so that they might take advantage of the financial manna I represented, and in larger extended households comprising several
agnatically related men and their in-marrying wives, preferential treatment,
ruptures, and family divisions may readily be attributed to the action of witches.
Several older women in the village, normally widows, were also supposed to be
adept at concocting love potions and their hand was frequently discerned in surprising matches, particularly hypergamous ones—i.e., where the woman marries
up. Misfortune was also sometimes attributed to witchcraft, notably with ailing
livestock, and a good many accidents and the like were chalked down to the evil

---

16. I can neither read nor competently speak classical Arabic and Al-Qarafi's *Differences*
(*Al-Furuq*) is untranslated. My Moroccan friends assure me that this is what he says
in this passage. The French language blogosphere agrees.

eye (Ṭit), which is locally supposed to work without intent,[17] but which is none-theless a form of magical action that typically strikes from within a community.

Ideas of witchcraft, then, are common in the area and sink their roots into prevailing infrastructures of intimacy such as friendship, kinship, and coresi-dence; they do not, however, have either the discursive scope or intensity of their equivalents in parts of sub-Sahara Africa, or indeed elsewhere in Morocco. Such at least is my experience, and there is admittedly an extent to which it is under-determined by the fact that I am a man, with limited access to all-female gath-erings, and witchcraft and magic are very much female domains of concern—it is women who are generally supposed to be witches, they who typically make use of love philters, and most significantly they who discuss their fallout and make accusations. That being said, it is also true that though witchcraft is often evoked to explain strange occurrences, peculiar matches, or minor misfortune, it is scarcely ever given as an explanation for serious calamities like illness or death by either men or women (as is so common elsewhere). I worked intermittently as an interpreter in a medical clinic in the area for nearly a year, often alongside a local interpreter, and spent considerable time independently exploring local understandings of etiology—witchcraft was striking only by its absence.[18] To invoke a classic anthropological example, when local granaries collapse, as they periodically do, sometimes injuring people, this is not attributed to witchcraft, and when small children fall from them and injure themselves, it is because they were reckless or their parents insufficiently cautious.

So witches are present, but they are not the essential enemy. This too is un-surprising in a local context. Witchcraft and conspiracy may, as I have argued, draw on quite different (albeit often overlapping) social and imaginary infra-structures, but one thing they do share is a fundamental anti-occultist aesthetic: they claim to identify (and ideally combat) an invisible or hidden reality that determines and above all explains the visible course of events. They also share a focus on revelation: conspiracy theories, like the social sciences, aim to make the world pellucid by revealing the secret structures of existence, whilst witchcraft seeks to ferret out the actual individuals who embody danger. In a place like the

---

17. Some people are simply born with the evil eye and when they pay you or your loved ones a compliment, the envy or jealousy within them may cause misfortune to strike.

18. This can also be seen as part of a wider refusal to attribute causes to illness (cf. Carey 2010).

High Atlas, where opacity is not necessarily seen as a problem, but rather embraced as a source of independence, this anti-occultist aesthetic cannot so easily gain social traction. What is more, witchcraft, as Geschiere so convincingly argues, is tied up not only with intimacy, but also by extension with betrayal, and in the High Atlas, as we saw in chapter 2, betrayal by intimates is, if not accepted, at least often tolerated as part and parcel of social existence. This explicit embrace of mistrust in the Moroccan High Atlas, along with its particular infrastructural environment, means that neither the witch nor the conspirator takes center stage in the region. Instead, fear and mistrust are invested in a third figure: the thief (*amkhar*).

INFRASTRUCTURES OF UNCERTAINTY

The *amkhar* is the great bogeyman of the Atlassian world. First and foremost in the straightforward acceptance of the word. People are inordinately worried about thieving. Some of this is probably justified: the material poverty of the central High Atlas is crushing and opportunistic petty theft of food, crops, or small and useful objects is rife. Accordingly, the village arranges for watchmen to guard the walnut trees when they are ripe and people keep their grain and valuables securely locked away. Much of the fear, though, seems faintly absurd to an outsider. I lived in an isolated building near the top of the village, halfway up a mountain and in plain sight of most of the houses. One day, I had been working on my roof and I left my ten-foot ladder leant against the wall while I went down to the shops to buy cigarettes. On the way, five villagers separately stooped and admonished me for being so foolhardy: somebody might steal the ladder. My objections, that if they and everybody else had noticed the ladder, it might be hard for a thief to make off with it unnoticed across the bare mountainside, were simply swept aside. Thieves were everywhere and they might pilfer anything.

An *amkhar*, however, is more than just a thief; he can also double up as a murderer. In fact, so congruent are the two notions that I do not even know a separate Tashelhiyt term for murderer ..., or bandit, or hoodlum. They are all thieves and any other damage they might do you is just an elaboration of their main line of work. This incarnation of the *amkhar* is also constantly on people's lips and no solitary journey, no nocturnal assignment, and no impromptu visit can occur without his being invoked. For example, when men had arranged to come to my house for a late-night dinner party (*zzerda*), I would leave the door on the latch to avoid repeatedly having to get up and let them in. And like clockwork, they would burst in, one after the other, often brandishing a blunt knife, and say "Aha! What if I had been an *amkhar*? I could have slit your throat. You should be more careful." In other words, they had all systematically checked whether the door was bolted *before* knocking, just so they could drive home their point about the perils of thieves.

Finally, the *amkhar* is also a cheat and a swindler: for instance, if you look at another man's hand when playing cards, then you have "robbed him" (*tukkert-as*), regardless of whether any money changed hands. And it is in this capacity that he most clearly populates the local imaginary of mistrust. The valleys of the Atlas are alive with tales of men who went to the plains and were hoodwinked by confidence tricksters. One story will suffice:

> *A man from a distant village [it's always a distant village] sold up the family lands and set out for Marrakech to deliver his share of the proceeds to his migrant brother. He wrapped up the money in a rug and put the rug in a sack, then he caught a bus to the city. When he arrived in the city, he immediately climbed into a taxi, determined to deliver the money directly to his brother. He gave the taxi driver the address and they set off. The driver looked at the nervous man in the rearview mirror and said,* "I bet you have something valuable there. You have to be careful; Marrakech is full of thieves." *The ingenuous mountaineer admitted that he was indeed carrying a great deal of money and that he was anxious to get to his brother's house. Unfortunately, the taxi driver could not find the address. They drove around for a bit and then the call to prayer resounded. The driver suggested that they should stop to pray and then resume their search. The poor mountaineer said* "But what about my bag?" *and the taxi driver reassured him that they would go to a mosque he knew and leave the bag with the imam. The man assented and they did so. After prayer, the man recovered his bag and the taxi driver drove him to his brother's house, which turned out to be not so hard to find. But when the poor man opened the bag, the money was gone.*

This was told to me as a cautionary tale, demonstrating the naïveté of villagers, the rapacity of the city, and the veracity of the oft repeated adage, *ur tilli tiqqa* (there is no trust): even a man of God may be a thief. But it also illustrates what I think is the key characteristic of the thief: his capacity to extract knowledge from the victim. As one friend put it, "*tkshm taḥramit g tamkhart, dima*" (there is always an element of ruse/cunning in theft). Indeed, what stands out in this tale is that the taxi driver "read" the victim and then found out what was in the bag. This idea of the theft of knowledge is further reflected in the more or less light-hearted and very frequent use of the term *amkhar* to describe somebody (often an anthropologist) who learned or discovered things about people and places. I was a "language-thief" (*amkhar n wawal*) for learning Tashelhiyt, a thief when I knew who was related to whom, and I was a thief when I mentioned some piece of local gossip to which I shouldn't have been privy. You rob someone when you find something out about them. And this is the primary characteristic that unites the tales told of ingenuous mountaineers in the city: not that they were simply robbed of their material possessions (although that is, of course, important), but that they were first relieved of the knowledge that made that possible. The thief, insofar as he inhabits the mistrusting imagination, is in large part a thief of knowledge, somebody who unveils and discovers things.

It is in this characteristic that the fundamental aesthetic difference between discourses of theft, witchcraft, and conspiracy consists. As we have seen, both witchcraft and conspiracy (as well as social science) share an anti-occultist aesthetic of revelation. The danger is hidden and it must be exposed. This is also true, up to a point, of the *amkhar*. He, too, is a figure who lurks in the dark, who sneaks away without taking leave (*irrwl zund amkhar*), who preys on people from the shadows. But this is not, in fact, his principal *modus operandi*, nor that aspect of his behavior that inspires the greatest fear and generates the greatest mistrust; to the contrary, the essential threat he poses is the capacity to cozen the truth out of his victims, to make that which is hidden plain. In a place where local people's inner worlds are held to be unreadable, their motives and intentions unsoundable, and knowledge about others has the potential to intrude on their autonomy, then it stands to reason that the mistrusting imagination primarily attaches itself not to the hidden figure of conspirator or witch, but to the one who discovers and reveals. In a non-transparent world whose very obscurity is the guarantor of freedom, the enemy is the Inquisitorial figure who pries out the truth. This enemy dwells neither in the bureaucratic infrastructure that houses conspiracy, nor the intimate social infrastructure of witchcraft, but in an abstract infrastructure of distributed knowledge that enables society, but imperils privacy and so independence and freedom.

On a final note, this provides an interesting parallel with the distributed data network that now subtends modernity in the form of the internet—a world in which the knowledge thief, in the form of the hacker, the whistleblower, or the multinational, is emerging as a new bogeyman and in which the Enlightenment goals of transparency and revelation run up against the desire for secrecy and obscurity. Precisely how this complex sociological constellation overlaps with the conspiratorial imaginary is something that doubtless merits further attention.

Conclusion

Over the course of this book, I have tried to show how mistrust can emerge at the confluence of particular ideas of personhood, practices of communication, and conceptions of the limits of knowledge. Where other people cannot be psychologically reduced or synthesized, where speech is labile and knowledge uncertain, mistrust is an appropriate attitude to adopt. This has significant implications for human relations, both intimate and distant. Whilst it does not necessarily sap or sever them, it does imprint them with a particular tenor. I focused on friendships, which I argued are not about disclosure and the blurring of personal or moral boundaries, but recognize and embrace the alterity of others as both a source of risk and pleasure. This mistrust at the heart of human relations also affects collective activity and political practice. It is the fundamental unreliability and untrustworthiness of others that gives rise to a political sphere predicated on ephemerality and contingency, one that is oriented toward the concrete and eschews abstract concepts of the good. Lastly, I looked at the different ways in which mistrust manifests itself in the form of fear, suggesting that the aesthetic of mistrust is always entwined with its infrastructural environment. In places regimented by bureaucracy, conspiracy theories find fertile ground; infrastructures of intimacy like kinship or neighborliness are conducive to ideas of witchcraft; and the distributed knowledge systems of the High Atlas are reflected in fears of the thief of knowledge.

By way of a conclusion, I would like very briefly to address two obvious lacunæ of my approach: religion and economics. Islam is the quiet canvas of large swathes of Atlassian life. It may lack the ostentation and spectacle of religion in the plains, from ecstatic brotherhoods to neofundamentalists, but it nonetheless structures patterns of everyday sociality, punctuates speech, and provides a collective frame for existence. And this frame was, at least until recently, strikingly homogeneous: until the arrival *en masse* of revivalist Islam in the mid-2000s, there were no great schismatic or doctrinal differences in the upper reaches of the mountains where I worked. Religion did not divide, but federate. Despite this, it did not appear to generate much in the way of trust. This is reflected in oral narrative genres: nigh on half of local fairytales and legends in the region involve the village community swindling the imam or vice versa. Shared faith was not seen as a guarantee of fidelity.

The question of trust in God is equally nice. On a superficial level, one could simply say that submission (*islām*) is quite different to trust and leave it at that, but there is also a slightly subtler and more speculative point to be made. As we have seen, in some parts of the (Christian) world, God may now be described as people's "best friend" and Jesus has long been considered an intimate companion; this is decidedly not the case in the High Atlas. Such an anthropomorphic representation of God, and one that assumed he could be known, would have been tantamount to blasphemy. This is because man's relationship of identity with God is quite different from that of Christian modernity. In the wake of the Inquisition (and later the Enlightenment), Christians, and those influenced by Christian epistemologies, can conceive of themselves as fashioned in God's image by virtue of their capacity to pierce to the truth of things or people—to sound reality. In the High Atlas, as in Islam more generally, people may not be understood as fashioned in God's likeness, but they do share some of his attributes in attenuated form. What they share, though, is not his ability to see through to the truth of his things, but his ultimate inscrutability. This is no basis for trust.

The situation is somewhat different as regards economic activity. I have not addressed it directly because it is the aspect of local life about which I know least. This is partly because, as I have repeatedly described, people lie and obfuscate when it comes to personal information, making it hard to get a clear picture of financial flows. It is also because there is little in the way of trade. Most families in the area generate the bulk of their meager income from livestock, cashcropping walnuts and iris roots, sharecropping, or remittances from the plains. None of these require sustained relations of trust: livestock and crops are periodically sold at markets; sharecropping is directly overseen by the landowners (who usually help harvest); and cash remittances are periodically delivered by hand, if they are delivered at all. There are, however, a small number of local men who do engage in trade or mount joint economic ventures, like running a minibus service to the plains or managing a hostel. And it is here, if anywhere, that people must, I think, develop strategies and build relationships of trust. And so this book, devoted to extolling mistrust from its lowly lie and presenting it as a legitimate object in its own right, might also paradoxically serve as a prelude to an exploration of the contours of trust in a trustless social world.

I began this book by claiming that each of the human and social sciences separately insisted that its very object of study was dependent on trust. And whilst this is certainly true of sociology, economics, political science, and to an extent linguistics, it is in fact a poor representation of the state of affairs in anthropology. With the exception of some work in economic anthropology inspired by the writings of Mark Granovetter on the embeddedness of economic relations in social networks (1985), there has been little systematic effort within the discipline to tackle trust directly or to address the thorny questions surrounding the relationship between trust and difference. What is the range and variety of possible conceptual bases for trust? How do these interact with ideas of personhood, collectives, and social relations? What kind of epistemological commitment does trust entail? Perhaps mistrust would be a good place to start looking for answers to these questions.

References

Abelès, M. 1995. "Pour une anthropologie des institutions." *L'Homme* 35 (135): 65–85.

Abrahams, R. D. 1964. *Deep down in the jungle: Negro narrative folklore from the streets of Philadelphia*. Hatboro, Pa.: Folklore Associates.

Adams, R., and G. Allan. 1998. *Placing friendship in context*. Cambridge: Cambridge University Press.

Agamben, G. 1995. *Homo Sacer. Il potere sovrano e la nuda vita*. Rome: Einaudi.

Aguilar, J. 1984. Trust and exchange: Expressive and instrumental dimensions of reciprocity in a peasant community. *Ethos* 12 (1): 3–29.

Albrow, M. 1970. *Bureaucracy*. London: Palgrave Macmillan.

Alès, C. 2000. "Anger as a marker of love: The ethics of conviviality among the Yanomami." In *The anthropology of love and anger: The aesthetics of conviviality in Native Amazonia*, edited by J. Overing and A. Passes, 133–51. London: Routledge.

Algan, Y., P. Cahuc, and A. Zylberberg. 2012. *La fabrique de la défiance*. Paris: Albin Michel.

Allard, O. 2010. "Bureaucratic anxiety: Asymmetrical interactions and the role of documents in the Orinoco Delta, Venezuela." *Hau: Journal of Ethnographic Theory* 2 (2): 234–56.

———, M. Carey, and R. Renault. 2016. "De l'art de se méfier," *Tracés* 31: 7–20.

al-Qarafi, Shihab al-Din, 1347H. *Kitab al-Furuq*, Vol. 4. Kaherah: Dar Ihya' al-Kutub al-'Arabiyyah.

Amahan, A. 1998. *Mutations sociales dans le Haut Atlas: les Ghoujdama*. Paris: La Maison des Sciences de l'Homme.

Aquinas, Thomas, St. 1265–1274. *Summa Theologica*.

Aragon, L. 1980. *Le mentir-vrai*. Paris: Gallimard.

Arendt, H. 1951. *The origins of totalitarianism*. New York: Schocken.

Aristotle. 1999. *Politics*. Kitchener, Ont.: Batoche Books.

Austin, J. L. 1962. *How to do things with words*. Cambridge: Harvard University Press.

Axelrod, R. 1984. *The evolution of cooperation*. New York: Basic Books.

Bajuk, T. 1999. "Udbomafija and the Rhetoric of Conspiracy." In *Paranoia within reason: A casebook on conspiracy as explanation*, edited by G. E. Marcus. Chicago: University of Chicago Press.

Bakhtin, M. 1981. *The dialogic imagination: Four essays*. Austin: University of Texas Press.

Banfield, E. C. 1958. *The moral basis of a backward society*. New York: Free Press.

Barkun, M. 2003. *A culture of conspiracy: Apocalyptic visions in contemporary America*. Berkeley and Los Angeles: University of California Press.

Barruel, A. 1797–1798. *Mémoires pour servir à l'histoire du jacobinisme (5 vol.)*. Hamburg: P. Fauche.

Beck, U. 1992. *Risk society: Towards a new modernity*. New Delhi: Sage.

Bell, S., and S. Coleman. 1999. *The anthropology of friendship*. Oxford: Berghahn.

Berque, J. 1955. *Structures sociales du Haut-Atlas*. Paris: Presses universitaires de France.

Bloch. M. 2015. "Durkheimian anthropology and religion: Going in and out of each other's bodies." *Hau: Journal of Ethnographic Theory* 5 (3): 285–99.

Bok, S. 1978. *Lying: Moral choice in public and private life*. New York: Pantheon Books.

Boltanski, L. 2012. *Enigmes et complots*. Paris: Gallimard.

———, and L. Thévenot. 1987. *De la justification. Les économies de la grandeur*. Paris: Gallimard.

Borgonovi, F. 2012. "The relationship between education and levels of trust and tolerance in Europe." *British Journal of Sociology* 63 (1): 146–67. 397 146..167

Bourdieu, P. 1980. "Le capital social. Notes provisoires," *Actes de la recherche en sciences sociales*, 31 (1): 2–3.

Brain, R. 1976. *Friends and lovers*. New York: Basic Books.

Bratich, J. 2008. *Conspiracy panics: Political rationality and popular culture*, Albany: State University of New York Press.

Bulut, E. 2005. "Tempête de Métal: le nationalisme populaire et ses peurs." *La Vie des Idées* 5: 47–56.

Candea, M. 2016. "De deux modalités de comparaison en anthropologie sociale." *L'Homme* 218: 183–218.

———, and G. da Col. 2012. "The return to hospitality." *Journal of the Royal Anthropological Institute* 18 (s1): 1–19.

Carey, M. 2007. "Ephemeral institutions: Practical anarchy in the Moroccan High Atlas." PhD thesis, Cambridge University.

——— 2010. "La folie mise en marge: Genre et aliénation chez les Berbères Ichelhiyn du Maroc." *Cahier d'Etudes Africaines* 205: 217–36.

——— 2012. "'The rules' in Morocco? Pragmatic approaches to flirtation and lying." *Hau: Journal of Ethnographic Theory* 2 (2): 188–205.

——— 2013. "Apolitical 'Islamisation'? On the limits of religiosity in montane Morocco." In *Articulating Islam: Anthropological approaches to Muslim worlds*, edited by M. Marsden and K. Retsikas, 193–208. Berlin: Springer.

Carrier, J. G. 1999. "People who can be friends: selves and social relationships." In *The anthropology of friendship*, edited by Sandra Bell and Simon Coleman. Oxford: Berghahn.

Carsten, J. (ed.). 2000. *Cultures of relatedness: New approaches to the study of kinship*. Cambridge: Cambridge University Press.

Casagrande, J. B. 1960. *In the company of man: Twenty portraits by anthropologists*. New York: Harper and Brothers.

Clastres, P. 1962. "Échange et pouvoir: philosophie de la chefferie indienne." *L'Homme* 2 (1): 51–65.

——— 1974. *La société contre l'Etat. Recherches d'anthropologie politique*. Paris: Minuit.

Cofta, P. 2007. *Trust, complexity and control: Confidence in a convergent world*. Hoboken, N.J.: Wiley.

Comaroff J., and J. L. Comaroff. 2003. "Transparent fictions; or, the conspiracies of a liberal imagination: An afterword." In *Transparency and conspiracy*, edited by H. G. West and T. Sanders. Durham, N.C.: Duke University Press.

Cook, K. S. (ed.). 2001. *Trust in Society*. New York: Russell Sage Foundation.

Course, M. 2010. "Making friends, making oneself: Friendship and the Mapuche person." In *The ways of friendship: Anthropological perspectives*, edited by E. Killick and A. Desai. Oxford: Berghahn Books.

Crapanzano, V. 1980. *Tuhami: Portrait of a Moroccan*. Chicago: University of Chicago Press.

da Col, G. 2012. "The poisoner and the parasite: Cosmoeconomics, fear, and hospitality among Dechen Tibetans." *Journal of the Royal Anthropological Institute* 18 (1): 175–95.

Danziger, E. 2010. "On trying and lying: Cultural configurations of the Gricean maxim of quality." *Intercultural Pragmatics* 7 (2): 199–219.

de Vienne, E. 2012. "'Make yourself uncomfortable': Joking relationships as predictable uncertainty among the Trumai of Central Brazil." *Hau: Journal of Ethnographic Theory* 2 (2): 163–87.

Dean, J. 1998. *Aliens in America: Conspiracy cultures from outerspace to cyberspace*. Ithaca, N.Y.: Cornell University Press.

Deleuze. G. 1968. *Différence et répétition*. Paris: Presses universitaires de France.

Descola, P. 1988. "La chefferie amérindienne dans l'anthropologie politique." *Revue française de science politique* 38 (5): 818–27.

Dodier, N. 1993. *L'expertise médicale—Essai de sociologie sur l'exercice du jugement*. Paris: Métailié.

Dunn, J. 1988. "Trust and political agency." In *Trust: Making and Breaking Cooperative Relations*, edited by D. Gambetta, 73–93. New York: Basil Blackwell.

Duranti, A. 2015. *The anthropology of intentions: Language in a world of others*. Cambridge: Cambridge University Press.

———, and C. Goodwin. 1992. *Rethinking context: Language as an interactive phenomenon*. Cambridge: Cambridge University Press.

Durkheim, E. 1893. *De la division du travail social*. Paris: Félix Alcan.

Dwyer, K. 1982. *Moroccan dialogues: Anthropology in question*. Baltimore, Md.: John Hopkins University Press.

Eickelman, D. F. 1976. *Moroccan Islam: Tradition and society in a pilgrimage center*. Austin: University of Texas Press.

El Mountassir, A. 2004. *Amarg: chants et poésies amazighs (Sud-Ouest du Maroc)*. Paris: L'Harmattan.

Engels, F. 2004 [1884]. *The origin of the family, private property and the state*. Chippendale, N.S.W.: Resistance Books.

Evans-Pritchard, E. 1940. *The Nuer: A description of the modes of livelihood and political institutions of a Nilotic people*. Oxford: Clarendon Press.

Faubion, J. D. 2001. *The shadows and lights of Waco: Millennialism today*. Princeton, N.J.: Princeton University Press.

Fausto, C. 2012. "The friend, the enemy, and the anthropologist: hostility and hospitality among the Parakanã (Amazonia, Brazil)." *Journal of the Royal Anthropological Institute* 18: 196–209.

Favret-Saada, J. 1977. *Les mots, la mort, les sorts: La sorcellerie dans le bocage.* Paris: Gallimard.

――― 2015. *The Anti-Witch.* London: Hau Books.

―――, and J. Contreras. 1981. *Corps pour corps: Enquête sur la sorcellerie dans le bocage.* Paris: Gallimard.

Featherstone, M. 2001. "The obscure politics of conspiracy theory." In *The age of anxiety: Conspiracy theory and the human sciences*, edited by J. Parish and M. Parker. Oxford: Blackwell.

Ferguson, J. 1994. *The anti-politics machine: 'Development', depoliticization and bureaucratic power in Lesotho.* Minneapolis: University of Minnesota Press.

Firth, R. 1967. *Tikopia ritual and belief.* Boston: Beacon Press.

Foisneau, L. 2016. "La crainte des Roms: Pratiques romanès de la defiance." *Tracés* 31 (2): 87–108.

Foster, G. M. 1965. "Peasant society and the image of limited good." *American Anthropologist* n.s., 67 (2): 293–315.

Foucault, F. 1976. *Histoire de la sexualité I: La volonté de savoir.* Paris: Gallimard.

Frankfurt, H. 1986. "On bullshit." *Raritan Quarterly Review* 6 (2): 81–100.

Froerer, P. 2010. "Close friends: The importance of proximity in the formation of friendship in Chhattisgarh, India." In *The ways of friendship: Anthropological perspectives*, edited by E. Killick and A. Desai. Oxford: Berghahn Books.

Fukuyama, F. 1995. *Trust: The social virtues and the creation of prosperity.* London: Hamish Hamilton.

Gambetta, D. (ed.).1988. *Trust: Making and breaking cooperative relations.* Oxford: Basil Blackwell.

Garfinkel, H. 1963. "A conception of and experiments with 'trust' as a condition of stable concerted actions." In *Motivation and social interaction*, edited by O. J. Harvey, 187–238. New York: Ronald Press.

Geertz, C. 1980. *Negara: The theatre state in nineteenth-century Bali.* Princeton, N.J.: Princeton University Press.

―――, H. Geertz, and L. J. Rosen. 1979. *Meaning and order in Moroccan society: Three essays in cultural analysis.* Cambridge: Cambridge University Press.

Gellner, E. 1969. *Saints of the Atlas.* London: Weidenfeld & Nicolson.

Geschiere, P. 2013. *Witchcraft, intimacy and trust: Africa in comparison.* Chicago: University of Chicago Press.

Giddens, A. 1990. *The consequences of modernity*. Cambridge: Polity.

———— 1991. *Modernity and self-identity: Self and society in the late modern age.* Stanford, Calif.: Stanford University Press.

———— 1992. *The transformation of intimacy: Sexuality, love and eroticism in modern societies.* Stanford, Calif.: Stanford University Press.

Gilsenan, M. 1976. "Lying, Honor, and Contradiction." In *Transaction and meaning: Directions in the anthropology of exchange and symbolic behavior,* edited by B. Kapferer, 191–219. Philadelphia: Institute for the Study of Human Issues.

———— 1996. *Lords of the Lebanese marches: Violence and narrative in an Arab society.* London: I.B. Tauris.

Gottesman, A. 2014. *Politics and the street in democratic Athens.* Cambridge: Cambridge University Press.

Govier, T. 1997. *Social trust and human communities.* Montreal: McGill-Queen's University Press.

Graeber, D. 2004. *Fragments of an anarchist anthropology.* Chicago: Prickly Paradigm Press.

Granovetter, M. 1985. "Economic action and social structure: The problem of embeddedness." *American Journal of Sociology* 91 (3): 481–510.

Grant, B. 1999. "The return of the repressed: Conversations with three Russian entrepreneurs." In *Paranoia within reason: A casebook on conspiracy as explanation,* edited by G. E. Marcus, 241–68. Chicago: University of Chicago Press.

Grice, P. 1969. "Utterer's meaning and intentions." *The Philosophical Review* 78: 144–77.

———— 1975. "Logic and Conversation." *Syntax and Semantics* 3: 41–58.

Griswold, C. L. 1999. *Adam Smith and the virtues of the Enlightenment.* New York: Cambridge University Press.

Guerreiro, A. 2015. "Political chimeras: The uncertainty of the chief's speech in the Upper Xingu." *Hau: Journal of Ethnographic Theory* 5 (1): 59–85.

Gulliver, P. H. 1971. *Neighbours and networks: The idiom of kinship in social action among the Ndendeuli of Tanzania.* Berkeley and Los Angeles: University of California Press.

Haiman, J. 1998. *Talk is cheap: Sarcasm, alienation, and the evolution of language.* New York: Oxford University Press.

Hammoudi, A. 1988. *La victime et ses masques: Essai sur le sacrifice et la mascarade au Maghreb.* Paris: Seuil.

———— 1997. *Master and disciple: The cultural foundations of Moroccan authoritarianism.* Chicago: University of Chicago Press.

Hanoteau, A., and A. Letourneux. 1872–73. *La Kabylie et les coutumes kabyles.* Paris: Augustin Challamel.

Harari, Y. N. 2014. *Sapiens: A brief history of humankind.* London: Harvill Secker.

Hardin, R. 2001. "Concepts and explanations of trust." In *Trust in Society,* edited by K. S. Cook, 3–39. New York: Russell Sage Foundation.

———— 2004. *Trust and trustworthiness.* New York: Russell Sage Foundation.

———— 2006. *Trust.* Cambridge: Polity.

Hart, D. M. 1976. *The Aith Waryaghar of the Moroccan Rif: An ethnography and history.* Tucson: University of Arizona Press.

———— 1981. *Dadda 'Atta and his forty grandsons: The socio-political organisation of the Ait 'Atta of Southern Morocco.* Cambridge: Middle East and North African Studies Press.

Heins, V. 2007. "Critical theory and the traps of conspiracy thinking." *Philosophy & Social Criticism* 33 (7): 787–801.

Herzfeld, M. 1987. "'As in your own house': Hospitality, ethnography, and the stereotype of Mediterranean society." In *Honor and Shame and the Unity of the Mediterranean,* edited by D. D. Gilmore. Washington, D.C.: American Anthropological Association.

Hoffman, K. 2007. *We share walls: Language, land, and gender in Berber Morocco.* Malden, Mass.: Blackwell Publishing.

Hofstadter, R. 2008 [1964]. *The paranoid style in American politics.* New York: Vintage Books.

Holbraad, M. 2012. *Truth in motion: The recursive anthropology of Cuban divination.* Chicago: University of Chicago Press.

Hollan, D., and J. C. Throop. 2008. "Whatever happened to empathy? Introduction." *Ethos* 36 (4): 475–89.

———— and ———— 2011. "The anthropology of empathy: Introduction." In *The anthropology of empathy: Experiencing the lives of others in Pacific societies,* edited by D. W. Hollan and J. C. Throop. Oxford: Berghahn Books.

Hume, D. 1738. *A treatise of human nature.* London: John Noon.

Humphrey, C. 2010. "Odessa: Pogroms in a cosmopolitan city." *Ab Imperio* 4: 1–53.

————, and S. Skvirskaja (eds.). 2012. *Post-cosmopolitan cities: Explorations of urban coexistence.* Oxford: Berghahn Books.

Hymes, D. H. 1983. *Essays in the history of linguistic anthropology*. Philadelphia: John Benjamins Publishing.

James, N. 2001. "Taking conspiracy seriously: Fantastic narratives and Mr Grey the Pan-Afrikanist on Montserrat." In *The age of anxiety: Conspiracy theory and the human sciences*, edited by J. Parish and M. Parker. Oxford: Blackwell.

Janmaat, J. G. 2010. "Classroom diversity and its relation to tolerance, trust and participation in England, Sweden and Germany." LLAKES Research Paper 4. Available at: https://germjanmaat.files.wordpress.com/2010/02/diversi-tyllakes.pdf (accessed August 21, 2017).

Kartzow, M. 2009. *Gossip and gender: Othering of speech in the pastoral epistles*. New York: Walter de Gruyter.

Keane, W. 2008. "Others, other minds, and others' theories of other minds: An afterword on the psychology and politics of opacity claims." *Anthropological Quarterly* 81 (2): 473–82.

——— 2017. *Ethical life: Its natural and social histories*. Princeton, N.J.: Princeton University Press.

Keeley, B. 1999. "Of conspiracy theories." *Journal of Philosophy* 96 (3): 109–26.

Keenan, E. O. 1976. "The universality of conversational postulates." *Language in Society* 5: 67–80.

Killick, E. 2010. "Ayompari, compadre, amigo: Forms of fellowship in Peruvian Amazonia." In *The ways of friendship: Anthropological perspectives*, edited by E. Killick and A. Desai. Oxford: Berghahn Books.

Knight, P. 2000. *Conspiracy culture: From Kennedy to the X-Files*. London: Routledge.

Kraus, W. 1998. "Contestable identities: Tribal structures in the Moroccan High Atlas. *Journal of the Royal Anthropological Institute* 4 (1): 1–22.

Lacroix, T. 2003. "Les réseaux marocains d'aide au développement." *Hommes et migrations* 1242: 121–128.

Lahoussain, J. 2003. "L'expérience de l'association migration et développement au Maroc." In *Coopérer au début du XXIe siècle. Pourquoi? Comment? Questions sans préjugés*, 247–50. Paris: Karthala.

Latour, B. 2004. "Why has critique run out of steam? From matters of fact to matters of concern." *Critical Inquiry* 30: 225–48.

Laudun, J. 2012. "'Talking Shit' in Rayne: How esthetic features reveal ethical structures." *Journal of American Folklore* 125 (497): 304–26.

Lebner, A. B. 2012. "A Christian politics of friendship on a Brazilian frontier." *Ethnos* 77 (4): 496–517.

Leman, P. J., and M. Cinnirella. 2007. "A major event has a major cause: Evidence for the role of heuristics in reasoning about conspiracy theories." *Social Psychological Review* 9 (2): 18–28.

Levinson, S. C. 2000. *Presumptive meanings: The theory of generalized conversational implicature.* Cambridge: MIT Press.

Lewandowsky, S., G. E. Gignac, and K. Oberauer. 2013. "The role of conspiracist ideation and worldviews in predicting rejection of science." *PLoS ONE* 8(10): e75637.

Lowie, R. 1948. "Some aspects of political organization among the American aborigines." *Journal of the Royal Anthropological Institute* 78 (1–2): 11–24.

Luhmann, N. 1979. *Trust and power.* New York: John Wiley & Sons.

——— 1988. "Familiarity, confidence, trust: Problems and alternatives." In *Trust: Making and breaking cooperative relations,* edited by D. Gambetta, 94–107. New York: Basil Blackwell.

Macdonald, C. 2011. "Primitive anarchs: Anarchism and the anthropological imagination." *Social Evolution and History* 10 (2): 67–86.

Mahé, A. 2002. *Histoire de la Grande Kabylie. XIXe–XXe siècles. Anthropologie du lien social dans les communautés villageoises.* Paris: Bouchène.

Malinowski, B. 1935. *Coral gardens and their magic.* London: Routledge.

Marcus, G. E. (ed.). 1999. *Paranoia within reason: A casebook on conspiracy as explanation.* Chicago: University of Chicago Press.

Marsden, M. 2009. "A tour not so grand: Mobile Muslims in northern Pakistan." *Journal of the Royal Anthropological Institute* 15 (1): 57–75.

Marzano, M. 2010. *Le contrat de défiance.* Paris: Grasset.

Masqueray, E. 1886. *Formation des cités chez les populations sédentaires de l'Algérie: Kabyles du Djurdjura, Chaouiïa de l'Aourās, Beni Mezaāb.* Paris: E. Leroux.

Mauss, M. 1968 [1923–24]. *Essai sur le don: Forme et raison de l'échange dans les sociétés archaïques.* Paris: Presses Universitaires de France.

Mead, M. 1928. *Coming of age in Samoa: A psychological study of primitive youth for Western civilization.* New York: William Morrow.

Miliband, R. 1969. *The state in capitalist society.* London: Weidenfeld and Nicolson.

Misztal, B. 1996. *Trust in modern societies: The search for the bases of social order.* Cambridge: Polity.

Möllering, G. 2002. "The nature of trust: From Georg Simmel to a theory of expectation, interpretation and suspension." *Sociology* 35 (2): 403–20.

Montagne, R. 1930. *Les Berberes et le Makhzen dans le Sud du Maroc: essai sur la transformation politique des Berberes sedentaires (groupe chleuh)*. Paris: Félix Alcan.

Moya, I. 2015. "Unavowed value: Economy, comparison, and hierarchy in Dakar." *Hau: Journal of Ethnographic Theory* 5 (1): 151–72.

Nederman, C. J. 2000. *Worlds of difference: European discourses of toleration, c. 1100–c. 1550*. University Park: Pennsylvania State University Press.

Obeid, M. 2010. "Friendship, kinship and sociality in a Lebanese town." In *The ways of friendship: Anthropological perspectives*, edited by E. Killick and A. Desai. Oxford: Berghahn Books.

Oliker, S. 1998. "The modernization of friendship: Individualism, intimacy and gender in the nineteenth century." In *Placing friendship in context*, edited by R. Adams and G. Allan. Cambridge: Cambridge University Press.

Oushakine, S. A. 2009. "'Stop the invasion!': Money, patriotism, and conspiracy in Russia." *Social Research: An International Quarterly* 76 (1): 71–116.

Paine, R. 1967. "What is gossip about? An alternative hypothesis." *Man* n.s. 2 (2): 278–85.

———— 1969. "In search of friendship: An exploratory analysis in 'middle-class' culture." *Man* n.s. 4 (4): 505–24.

Parish, J., and M. Parker (eds.) 2001. *The age of anxiety: Conspiracy theory and the human sciences*. Oxford: Blackwell.

Parker, M. 2001. "Human science as a conspiracy theory." In *The age of anxiety: Conspiracy theory and the human sciences*, edited by J. Parish and M. Parker. Oxford: Blackwell.

Parsons, T. 1978. *Action theory and the human condition*. New York: Free Press.

Pelkmans, M., and R. Machold. 2011. "Conspiracy theories and their truth trajectories." *Focaal: Journal of Global and Historical Anthropology* 59: 66–80.

Pipes, D. 1997. *Conspiracy: How the paranoid style flourishes and where it comes from*. New York: Touchstone.

Polanyi, K. 1944. *The great transformation: The political and economic origins of our time*. New York: Farrar and Rinehart.

Poundstone. W. 1992. *Prisoner's dilemma*. New York: Doubleday.

Premack, D., and G. Woodruff. 1978. Does the chimpanzee have a theory of mind? Behavioral and Brain Sciences 1 (4): 515–26.

Putnam, R. D. 1993. *Making democracy work: Civic traditions in modern Italy*. Princeton, N.J.: Princeton University Press.

———— 2000. *Bowling alone: The collapse and revival of American community.* New York: Simon and Schuster.

————, R. Leonardi, and R. Y. Nanetti. 1993. *Making democracy work: Civic traditions in modern Italy.* Princeton, N.J.: Princeton University Press.

Quinn, A. 2001. "Tout est lié: The front national and media conspiracy theories." In *The age of anxiety: Conspiracy theory and the human sciences*, edited by J. Parish and M. Parker. Oxford: Blackwell.

Rabinow, P. 1977. *Reflections on fieldwork in Morocco.* Berkeley and Los Angeles: University of California Press.

Rabo, A. 2014; "'It has all been planned': Talking about us and powerful others in contemporary Syria." In *Conspiracy theories in the United States and the Middle East: A comparative perspective*, edited by M. Butter and M. Reinkowski. Berlin: Walter de Gruyter.

Rachik, H. 2012. *Le proche et le lointain: Un siècle d'anthropologie au Maroc.* Marseille: Editions parenthèses.

Radi, S. 2013. *Surnaturel et société: L'explication magique de la maladie et du malheur à Khénifra, Maroc.* Rabat: Centre Jacques-Berque. Available at http://books.openedition.org/cjb/470 (accessed August 21, 2017).

Reedy, K. 2007. "A state of conspiracy: Syrian challenges to political authority in the course of the everyday." PhD thesis, University of Edinburgh.

Robbins, J. 2008. "On not knowing other minds: Confession, intention, and linguistic exchange in a Papua New Guinea community." *Anthropological Quarterly* 81 (2): 421–9.

———— 2013. "Beyond the suffering subject: Toward an anthropology of the good." *Journal of the Royal Anthropological Institute* 19 (3): 447–62.

Roberts, H. 2002. "Perspectives of Berber politics: On Gellner and Masqueray, or Durkheim's mistake." *Journal of the Royal Anthropological Institute* 8 (1): 107–26.

Rodgers, G. 2010. "Friendship, distance and kinship-talk amongst Mozambican refugees in South Africa." In *The ways of friendship: Anthropological perspectives*, edited by E. Killick and A. Desai. Oxford: Berghahn Books.

Rosaldo, M. Z. 1982. "The things we do with words: Ilongot speech acts and speech act theory in philosophy." *Language in Society* 11 (2): 203–37.

Rosanvallon, P. 2006. *La contre démocratie: La politique à l'âge de la défiance.* Paris: Le Seuil.

Rosen, L. 1989. *The anthropology of justice: Law as culture in Islamic society (Lewis Henry Morgan Lectures).* Cambridge: Cambridge University Press.

Rydgren, J., D. Sofi, and M. Hällsten 2013. "Interethnic friendship, trust, and tolerance: Findings from two north Iraqi cities." *American Journal of Sociology* 118 (6): 1650–94.

Sahlins, M. 2008. "The stranger-king or elementary forms of the politics of life." *Indonesia and the Malay World* 36 (105): 177–99.

Santos, G. D. 2008. "On 'same-year siblings' in rural South China." *Journal of the Royal Anthropological Institute* 14 (3): 535–53.

Sarraute, N. 1956. *L'ère du soupçon*. Paris: Gallimard.

Schieffelin, B. B. 2008. "Speaking only your own mind: Reflections on talk, gossip and intentionality in Bosavi." *Anthropological Quarterly* 81 (2): 431–41.

Scott, J. 1987. *Weapons of the weak: Everyday forms of peasant resistance*. New Haven: Yale University Press.

———— 2009. *The art of not being governed: An anarchist history of upland Southeast Asia*. New Haven: Yale University Press.

Seligman, A. 1997. *The problem of trust*. Princeton, N.J.: Princeton University Press.

———— 2011. "Trust, tolerance and the challenge of difference." *Comparative Sociology* 10: 337–57.

Senft, G. 2008. "The case: The Trobriand Islanders vs H. P. Grice: Kilivila and the Gricean maxims of quality and manner." *Anthropos* 103: 139–47.

Séveri, C., and J. Bonhomme (eds.). 2009. *Paroles en actes*. Paris: L'Herne.

Shack, W. A. 1963. "Religious ideas and social action in Gurage bond-friendship." *Africa* 33 (3): 198–208.

Silver, A. 1990. "Friendship in commercial society: Eighteenth-century social theory and modern sociology." *American Journal of Sociology* 95 (6): 1474–504.

Silverstein, P. A. 2002. "An excess of truth: Violence, conspiracy theorizing and the Algerian Civil War." *Anthropological Quarterly* 75 (4): 643–74.

Simenel, R. 2010. *L'origine est aux friontières. Les Aït Ba'amran, un exil en terre d'arganiers*. Paris: CNRS éditions; Editions de la Maison des Sciences de l'Homme.

Simmel, G. 1950. *The sociology of Georg Simmel*. New York: Free Press.

———— 1990. *The philosophy of money*. London: Routledge.

Simpson, J. A. 2007. "Psychological foundations of trust." *Current Directions in Psychological Science* 16 (5): 264–68.

Smith, A. 1976 [1776]. *An inquiry into the nature and causes of the wealth of nations*. Chicago: University of Chicago Press.

———— 2002 [1759]. *The theory of moral sentiments*. Cambridge: Cambridge University Press.

Soares, L. E. 1999. "A toast to fear: Ethnographic flashes and two quasi-aphorisms." In *Paranoia within reason: A casebook on conspiracy as explanation*, edited by G. E. Marcus, 225–40. Chicago: University of Chicago Press.

Song, H. 2012. "Cogito, mimesis, and conspiracy theory." *Culture, Theory and Critique* 53 (1): 1–18.

Spadolo, E. 2011. "Forgive me friend: Mohammed and Ibrahim." *Anthropological Quarterly* 84 (3): 737–56.

Stasch, R. 2008. "Knowing minds is a matter of authority: Political dimensions of opacity statements in Korowai moral psychology." *Anthropological Quarterly* 81 (2): 443–53.

Stewart, M. 1989. "'True speech': Song and the moral order of a Hungarian Vlach gypsy community." *Man* 24 (1): 79–102.

Strathern, M. 1985. "Discovering 'social control'." *Journal of Law and Society* 12 (2): 111–34.

———— 1988. *The gender of the gift*. Berkeley and Los Angeles: University of California Press.

Sullivan, J. L., J. Piereson, and G. E. Marcus. 1982. *Political tolerance and American democracy*. Chicago: University of Chicago Press.

Svendsen, G. T. and G. L. Svendsen (eds). 2009. *Handbook of social capital: The troika of sociology, political science and economics*. Cheltenham, UK: Edward Elgar Publishing.

Sztompka, P. 1999. *Trust: A sociological theory*. Cambridge: Cambridge University Press.

Tarde, G. 1902. *Psychologie économique*. Paris: Félix Alcan.

Turner, V. 1967. *In the forest of symbols: Aspects of Ndembu ritual*. Ithaca, N.Y.: Cornell University Press.

Walker, H. 2015. "Justice and the dark arts: Law and shamanism in Amazonia." *American Anthropologist* 117 (1): 47–58.

Weber, M. 1947. *The theory of social and economic organisation*. Edited by T. Parsons. London: Collier Macmillan.

Weinstein, J. R. 2013. *Adam Smith's pluralism: Rationality, education, and the moral sentiments*. New Haven: Yale University Press.

Wheelock, W. T. 1982. "The problem of ritual language: From information to situation." *Journal of the American Academy of Religion* 50: 49–71.

Wilde, G. 2009. *Religión y poder en las misiones de Guaraníes*. Buenos Aires: Editorial Sb.

Williams, M. T. 1991. *Washing "the great unwashed": Public baths in urban America*. Columbus: Ohio State University Press.

Wittgenstein, L. 2001 [1953]. *Philosophical investigations*. Oxford: Blackwell Publishing.

Woodburn, J. 1982. "Egalitarian societies." *Man* 17 (3): 431–51.

Index

aesthetic, 76, 86, 99, 107
    of bureaucracy, 95, 98
    of conspiracy, 92–93
    of revelation, 94, 102–105
alterity, 8–10, 107
Amazonia, 29n10, 51, 56, 65
Anarchism, 63–65, 78, 82
autonomy, 12, 29, 31–35, 82, 105
    as an idea, 31n14, 86
    and duplicity, 59
    and freedom, 45
    and interiority, 34–35
    as a philosophy, 10
    as a psychological phenomenon,
        31, 34
    and trust, 52
Ayt Aḥwash, 71, 73

betrayal, 3, 101, 103
    and friendship, 40–41, 45, 53, 58–61
    and witchcraft, 85, 99
    See also treachery
bureaucracy, 85, 95–99
    aesthetic of, 95, 98
    and bureaucratic imagination,
        91–98
    of the church, 96

and conspiracy theory, 12, 107
    infrastructure, 105
    Latin American 96
    Moroccan, 98
    and NGOs, 68
    postcolonial, 56

certainty
    and communication, 37
    infrastructures of, 103–106
    and proximity, 8
    and uncertainty, 27, 37
character, 6, 11, 29–34
civil society
    the bonds of, 47
    and the Enlightenment, 50, 52, 64
    and trust, 40
Clastres, Pierre, 65, 75, 76, 80
commercial relations, 47, 50–53
communication, 18, 33
    and conversation, 25, 28, 32, 36
    and cooperation, 24
    ontology of, 10
    practice of, 11
    and ritual, 25
    and trust, 1–3, 16
    and uncertainty, 37

confidence
and communication, 16
and friendship, 49
and systems, 5n8
and trust, 6, 15
conspiracy (theories)
and bureaucratic imagination, 12,
91–99, 105, 107
and witchcraft, 85–86, 102, 105
contingency, 63–65, 76–77, 80–83
cooperation, 3–5
and communication, 24
games, 4
organized, 66–69
patterns of, 63
principle of, 17–18
and trust, 64
council (village), 12, 67–80

democracy
and the individual, 64
and mistrust, 4n6
structures and imaginaries of
liberal democracy, 46, 55, 63
and village councils, 68
development (see also NGOs), 68

empathy, 48–49
Enlightenment (Scottish), 47, 49–52,
57, 64
ephemeral institutions, 12, 107
and powerlessness, 65
village councils as, 73, 78–81
equality/egalitarianism, 10, 39, 46–49,
79
in Cameroon, 100
and friendship, 47, 56–57
in immediate-return systems, 73
and opacity, 34n21
in South America, 76

falsehood, 16, 26–27, 33–36
familiarity, 6–9, 44, 46, 57
Favret-Saada, Jeanne, 100

forgiveness, 40, 58–61
friendship, 49–61
betrayed, 44–45
and kinship, 85, 98, 102
as an ordering principle, 40
representations and practices of,
11, 41
as a voluntary bond, 47

Geschiere, Peter, 99, 100, 103
God
forgiveness of, 61
and friendship, 51
and shepherds, 22
and trust, 6, 108
veiled by, 31
gossip, 3, 42, 105
as anthropological data, 30
and biga sopa, 24
among the Bosavi, 35n22
shunned by men, 21, 34
in Montegrano, 2
in the insular Pacific, 29
and truthfulness, 27
Graeber, David, 65, 77–80
Grice, Paul, 1, 16–19, 24–27, 33, 35

hermeneutic veil, 31, 35, 37
Hofstadter, Richard, 92–95
hospitality, 8, 45, 61

identification, 54n18, 59
as imaginative projection, 46–49
moral, 34n18
imagination, 85, 91–96, 105
implicature, 16–19, 24
individualism, 47–52, 57, 64
infrastructure
bureaucratic, 105
environmental, 85, 103
epistemological, 85
imaginary, 102
of intimacy, 96–103
of kinship, 101

organizational, 91
social, 86, 100, 105, 107
inner world
    inscrutability of others', 11, 28, 31,
        58, 105
    interrogation of others', 30
    participation in others', 48–49
inscrutability
    of God, 108
    of others' inner worlds, 11, 28,
        57n22, 86
intention
    and anarchism, 82
    and apophenia, 6
    Clastres on, 76, 80
    and mendacity, 27
    and mistrust, 8n11, 49n9
    other people's, 29–36, 105
interiority, 11, 28, 32–34
intimacy
    for anthropologists, 60
    in Chitral, 56n21
    social infrastructures of, 85,
        96–102
    and the inner self, 58
    on journeys, 57
    physical, 57
    and the Scottish Enlightenment,
        49
    and social life, 17, 30
    and strangers, 9
    and trustworthiness, 40–43, 52
    and witchcraft, 103
Ishelhiyn, 12, 28, 74
    and egalitarianism, 34
    and ritual life, 71n9

Kabylia, 65, 67, 75
kinship, 2, 7, 28, 52–57
    in economic life, 54
    and friendship, 55
    imaginary infrastructures of,
        101–102
    and mistrust, 27, 41n3, 85

and polity in the High Atlas,
    65–67, 98
severance of, 100
and witchcraft, 100
knowledge, 86, 104–107
Kulikovo Field, 87–90

liberal(ism)
    democratic, 40, 55, 46, 63
    modernity, 47, 52
    neoliberalism, 46
    as a social ideal, 39
    societies, 51–59
ljmā', (see council)
Luhmann, Niklas, 4–6, 15–16, 31, 83
lying/mendacity
    biga sopa, 24
    Grice on, 18
    and obfuscation, 11, 15–16
    as plausible falsehood, 26–28
    suspended veracity, 35–37

magic, 24, 101, 102
Mediterranean, 8, 20, 23
Melanesia, 11, 29, 54
Middle East
    conflagration in, 97
    conspiracy theories in, 91, 96
    ethnography of, 8
    loss of trust in, 93
    male sociability in, 20n4, 55
Mopan Maya, 20, 33
motives
    curiosity about, 29–32, 79
    hidden, 4, 11, 105

NGOs, 53, 74–75, 78–79

Odessa, 3, 86–90
opacity, 29, 34, 86, 103

participation, 48–49, 94
personality
    attribution of, 6, 29–31

knowability of, 10
magic and, 101
synthetic concept of, 32
pragmatism
  meta-pragmatism, 26, 35
  and political practice, 83
  and tradition, 19
  in understanding of speech, 11,
    26; 83
predictability
  and coalitions, 12
  and personality, 10
  of others' actions, 46, 58–59
  and proximity, 8
  of reality, 80
  and trust, 40
  and unknowability, 11
Realpolitik, 63, 65, 82
revelation
  aesthetic of, 86, 94, 105
  Enlightenment goal of, 106
  of the inner self, 58
  and witchcraft, 102, 105
Robbins, Joel, 28, 29, 83
Rosen, Lawrence, 28, 33, 35
Rumsey, Josh, 28

Scott, James, 65, 77, 79
segmentary lineage, 8, 65, 66
self-interest, 47
Silver, Allan, 40, 47–50, 58
Simmel, Georg, 1, 3–6, 9–10
Smith, Adam, 47–50, 53
social capital, 40, 46–47, 51–52
state
  and anarchism, 75–82
  and conspiracy theory, 95–98
  postcolonial, 56
  socialist, 64
  statelessness, 76–77
  Theatre-State, 50
strangers, 8–9, 23, 50
Strathern, Marilyn, 10, 29, 54
sympathy, 48–52, 57–59

Tashelhiyt, 12n17, 21–27, 103
  idiom, 58, 67n5, 97
  interactional styles, 23
  language thief, 105
  metaphors, 36–37
theft
  of knowledge, 12, 68, 105
  and witchcraft, 85–86
  in infrastructures of uncertainty,
    103–107
theory of mind, 32
tolerance
  as articulated sympathy, 47–53
  discursive, 52
  in friendship, 59
  in Odessa, 86–87, 90
  and trust, 39–47
transparency, 39, 46, 104–106
treachery, 39–45
tribe, 67, 72
Trobriand Islands, 20, 24–27, 35
truth
  and conspiracy theory, 93–94
  discursive, 17
  Grice on, 16
  lḥaqq, 74
  Rosen on, 28
  in speech and conversation, 23–28
  and suspended veracity, 35–37
  and trust, 39n1
  and witchcraft, 105

Ukraine
  on Kulikovo Field, 86–91
  mistrust in, 3, 12
uncertainty, *(see certainty)*
unpredictability (*see predictability*)

witchcraft
  and conspiracy theories, 85–86,
    99–105
  and revelation, 102, 105

Zzerda/zzewerda, 20, 22, 41, 104

HAU Books is committed to publishing the most distinguished texts in classic and advanced anthropological theory. The titles aim to situate ethnography as the prime heuristic of anthropology, and return it to the forefront of conceptual developments in the discipline. HAU Books is sponsored by some of the world's most distinguished anthropology departments and research institutions, and releases its titles in both print editions and open-access formats.

www.haubooks.com

Supported by
Hau-N. E. T.
Network of Ethnographic Theory

University of Aarhus – EPICENTER (DK)
University of Amsterdam (NL)
Australian National University – Library (AU)
University of Bergen (NO)
Brown University (US)
California Institute of Integral Studies (US)
University of Campinas (BR)
University of Canterbury (NZ)
University College London (UK)
University of Cologne – The Global South Studies Centre (DE)
and City Library of Cologne (DE)
University of Colorado Boulder Libraries (US)
Cornell University (US)
University of Edinburgh (UK)
The Graduate Institute – Geneva Library (CH)
University of Groningen (NL)
Harvard University (US)
The Higher School of Economics in St. Petersburg (RU)
Humboldt University of Berlin (DE)
Indiana University Library (US)
Johns Hopkins University (US)
University of Kent (UK)
Lafayette College Library (US)
London School of Economics and Political Science (UK)
Institute of Social Sciences of the University of Lisbon (PL)
Ludwig Maximilian University of Munich (DE)
University of Manchester (UK)
The University of Manchester Library (UK)
Max-Planck Institute for the Study of Religious and Ethnic
Diversity at Göttingen (DE)
Musée de Quai Branly (FR)
Museu Nacional – UFRJ (BR)
Norwegian Museum of Cultural History (NO)
University of Oslo (NO)
University of Oslo Library (NO)
Princeton University (US)
University of Rochester (US)
SOAS, University of London (UK)
University of Sydney (AU)
University of Toronto Libraries (CA)

www.haujournal.org/haunet